CATCH BREAM

THE ANGLING TIMES LIBRARY

CATCH BREAM

WITH

JOHN WILSON

B⬢XTREE

in association with
ANGLING TIMES

First published in the UK 1992
by Boxtree Limited, 36 Tavistock Street,
London WC2E 7PB

1 3 5 7 9 10 8 6 4 2

© (text and photographs) John Wilson 1992
© (illustrations) Boxtree Limited 1992

Illustrations by David Batten
Cover design by Dave Goodman/Millions Design
Design by Peter Ward
Editor Helen Douglas-Cooper

Set in 10/13pt Linotron Bembo
Typeset by Cambrian Typesetters, Frimley
Colour origination by Fotographics, Hong Kong
Printed and bound in the UK by Richard Clay, Bungay

A catalogue record for this book is available
from the British Library.

ISBN 1 85283 151 0

AUTHOR'S ACKNOWLEDGEMENTS
No angling writer can produce a book without considerable
help from others. Allow me therefore to thank the editing
and design team, the mates who leave their own fishing to
photograph me, and a very special thank you to good
friend Dave Batten who has made such a fine job of the line
drawings.

CONTENTS

INTRODUCTION 7

THE SPECIES 9

ABOUT BREAM 15

LOCATING BREAM 21

TACKLE 36

BAITS 58

TECHNIQUES AND RIGS 76

INDEX 126

INTRODUCTION

BREAM have not become one of the most popular of our freshwater species by accident. When young, they graze the bottom in massive shoals like cows over a grassy field, and being easy to catch on light float tackle, create enjoyment for youngsters, pleasure anglers and match fishermen alike.

When those same bream reach adulthood, the size of the shoal will have greatly diminished through natural causes, and eventually only a group of specimens will remain. In waters where the natural food larder is poor, or where bream must compete with other, more aggressive species such as carp, adult bream will reach around the 5 lb mark. In a rich environment, on the other hand, where the bream enjoy minimal competition for the available food, a weight exceeding 10 lb is not out of the ordinary.

This book, however, is not about catching monsters. It covers the multitude of baits, groundbaits, tackle and techniques that you might like to use in a cross-section of waters where bream are most likely to be found. And to this end the fascinating subjects of location and habitat are extensively covered.

Although stillwater bream are not powerful fighters compared to tench and carp, in terms of sheer size even a 4 lb bream looks like a large fish, and their weight is often greatly over-estimated by the inexperienced. So what they lack in one area is made up for in another. Because the bream averages a fair size, and because it feeds avidly at night, it is much sought after during summer and autumn by a large proportion of pleasure and holiday fishermen. These anglers are only too pleased to swap the comfort of a warm bed to shiver by the water in the early hours of the morning, knowing they put at risk their married bliss for the opportunity to catch a netful.

CHAPTER ONE

THE
SPECIES

BREAM
(Abramis brama)

The bream, or bronze bream as it is sometimes called, has
several nicknames, few of them complimentary. When
small, bream are characteristically thin in cross-section, and
are often referred to as 'skimmers' or 'tin plates'. Bream
that live in heavily coloured lakes or pits, which turn pea-
green with phyto planktons during the summer due to
phosphate enrichment, may be called 'snotties' or 'slimies'.
This is due to the very thick protective layer of body
mucus or slime that the bream produces to coat its small,
flat scales in order to ward off parasites.

In coloured stillwaters the bream is a slow-moving,
ponderous, bottom-feeding fish – an easy target for all the
blood-sucking nasties, such as the transparent, flat-bodied
argulus and the double-sucker leeches inhabiting the
bottom detritus. Were it not for the protective mucus
layer, the bream would live a most uncomfortable life. In
clear water, whether running or still, the bream appear to
be more adept at out-running or evading potential parasites, and are covered with a noticeably thinner layer of
slime.

Bream living in clear waters are also much darker in
general coloration, especially in high water-temperature
conditions, but they lose this stark contrast during the
winter months. Adults are a distinct and beautiful slate
grey or dark bronze along the back, blending into shades
of burnished bronze along their deep flanks. The large,
deeply forked tail and the dorsal fin are dark blue-grey and
there is often a warm, mauve hue to the long anal fin. The
pelvic and pectoral fins are less coloured, and the belly is a
very pale creamy bronze.

The mature bream inhabiting heavily coloured fisheries

The bream's colour can vary considerably. Those living in coloured water are rather pale compared to the inhabitants of clear water, both still and moving. This typical fast-water river specimen, its flanks a deep bronze, has blue-grey fins and very little slime covering its scales.

is far less attractively coloured, having geared its camouflage to the density of the water in which it lives, so shades along the back can vary from pale grey or bronze to pale pewter on the flanks, blending into creamy off-white on the belly. The fins appear noticeably more translucent, tinted with hues of light grey. Whenever prolonged river flooding occurs, turning the water to the colour of milky tea, the bream pales even further to an overall wishy-washy, parchment colour.

SIZE

Whether living in clear or coloured, still or moving water, the bream is distinctly 'silvery' along the flanks during infancy, and exceptionally thin. Once adult, however, the bream is one of our longest cyprinids, with a potential length of up to 30 in, though most fully grown fish measure somewhere between 15 and 25 in.

As they mature, and depending on the richness and

quantity of natural food at their disposal, individual specimens grow to varying 'thicknesses' or 'widths'. This accounts for the enormous weight differential that often occurs between two bream that appear identical in length and depth. Owing to their immense body area, bream always look much heavier than they are and fishermen are caught out in their estimation of a bream's weight more often than with any other species.

With its characteristically deep body and pronounced hump, which rises from immediately behind the head to the leading ray of the dorsal fin, the bream is by far the deepest of our freshwater fish. The species has been so designed to enable large shoals to pack tightly together while feeding in close proximity, with just an inch or two between each fish and its neighbour.

The top weight in Europe, where it is a commercially produced food fish, is close on 20 lb, and while the bream record in British waters remained for many years at 13½ lb, this past decade has seen an unusual advance in the species' weight potential. Quite coincidentally, several stillwaters in different parts of England started producing

Adult bream in 4–5 lb class are the realistic goal from most fisheries in the British Isles. Yet in rich clear-water environments where competition species are few, weights of 8–9 lb and even 10 lb are not out of the question, as John proves by returning a brace of 'doubles' caught from a Norfolk gravel pit.

numbers of bream in excess of 12–13 lb from the mid-1980s. Queenford Lagoon in the Thames Valley, and meres, mostly in Cheshire, have produced the bulk of these massive bream of 14, 15 and even 16 lb, including the present record of 16 lb 6 oz taken by Anthony Bromley in 1986 from a Staffordshire mere.

Queenford Lagoon, the 70-acre gravel pit near Oxford, is the most famous big-bream water of all time, having produced during a 5-year period from 1985 to 1990 no less than fifty bream of 13½–16 lb. These statistics are even more staggering when you consider that each was over the old record. Prior to 1985 it took no less than 37 years for the bream record to be increased by just 1 oz, when the old record of 13 lb 8 oz, taken by E. Costin from Chidding-stone Castle Lake back in 1945, was beaten in 1982 by Mike Davison's fish of 13 lb 9 oz from Beeston Lake in Norfolk. This is an unprecedented situation in the realms of British record freshwater fish.

Enough of records and back to reality. In most fisheries throughout the British Isles, bream in the 4–5 lb class should be considered the realistic goal. If 6-, 7- or 8-pounders turn up, consider them a bonus.

Whenever bream shoal in vast numbers, the average adult weight will fall somewhere between 2 and 3½ lb, because with so many mouths to feed the competition for food is high. It is no rarity to encounter a shoal where all are like peas out of a pod. I can remember first experiencing this many years ago when I lived in North London, and travelled to the drains of Cambridgeshire on the regular coach outings run by the local club for my bream fishing. In those days, the club fished to the Thames or L.A.A. size limits, which prevented any bream under 12 in from being weighed in.

This was an effective rule, because immature fish did not end up in the keep-net, but had to be returned immediately. It was common, when fishing the coloured, slow-moving drains, to find a huge shoal of young bream in a swim, all of them seemingly under the 12-in size limit. And I was always fascinated, if not a trifle frustrated, by the sheer volume of 11-11½ in bream I caught without securing one to weigh in at the end of the day. To take thirty to fifty fish without one for the scales was not uncommon. However, they were all returned with the minimum of stress, and with luck they eventually matured into sizeable bream. There is probably a moral in this tale: bream wear less favourably than any other freshwater species when crammed into a keep-net, and had all those immature bream been taken to the scales, I am convinced that the eventual mortality rate would have been high.

These days, the large majority of southern clubs weigh 'all in', which may account for the fact that catches of immature bream are now nowhere near so common as they once were on all the more popular venues, in both still and running waters. In many fisheries there is, in fact, a 'reverse pyramid'. These fisheries contain a larger head of adult bream than they do of any other year-class except fry and fingerlings. Now, the reason for this phenomenon is certainly *not* all down to match fishing. In the richest, most mature lakeland and gravel-pit environments, which are rarely fished, entire populations of all year-classes between fry and adult bream are conspicuous by their absence. Farming chemicals, sewage effluent, winter run off (rivers), acid rain, habitat destruction by drainage departments, consecutive summers of poor fry recruitment due to unstable weather, and so on, all take their toll on young bream, which are extremely delicate fish.

All these factors added together probably explain why adult bream in so many fisheries now seem to attain far heavier weights than they once did. With far less competition for food from younger bream, or, in some cases (these waters produce the largest bream) a complete lack of intermediate-year classes, the adult bream enjoy a super-rich diet and consequently grow particularly thick in cross-section, increasing their expected weight potential by as much as one-third. Although this occurs all over the country, I know a number of waters in Norfolk, gravel pits mostly, which 15 to 20 years ago contained bream of all sizes, with the adult year-class, as one would expect, averaging 4–6 lb. Today in these same waters, where only that same adult year-class remains, individual specimens are topping 8–9 lb, with the occasional double-figure fish. It is a strange chain of events. And, of course, for these same bream to reach huge proportions, they must also live to a ripe old age. Certainly 20 to 25 years is nothing out of the ordinary, and it has been suggested that they could indeed live for very much longer under suitable conditions.

As with most cyprinids, it is not difficult to differentiate between the sexes. Look at the male bream on the right. It has a mass of white spawning tubercles covering its head, shoulders and pectoral fins during spawning time.

Clear-water bream are easy to locate with the aid of binoculars during the summer months, when they love to browse the warm, weedy shallows. At dusk and dawn they give away their position by porpoising through the surface film.

CHAPTER TWO

ABOUT BREAM

FEEDING

Like all cyprinids, the bream is equipped in the back of its throat with a pair of strong pharyngeal teeth, which it uses to chew its food into a pulp for swallowing. These teeth are responsible for the fisherman's maggots being returned as mere 'skins' on the hook, and for casters being crushed, because they squeeze out the juices very efficiently.

While the bream is most adept at sucking in baits suspended well above bottom, and even on the drop, it obtains most of its natural food through the protrusible mouth, which extends like a giant vacuum-hose to siphon up goodies, such as bloodworms and other insect larvae, annelid worms, molluscs and shrimps, from the bottom.

Wherever the bottom sediment is soft and easily disturbed, the change in water colour caused by shoals, especially large ones, feeding in earnest is very noticeable, and provides a wonderful visual pointer for their location. Bubbles, emitted through the bream's gills as a direct result of chewing, will rise to the surface, and be seen in the clouded water. Not the long fizzes of carp, nor in the quantity emitted by tench; just small groups containing several quite small bubbles. If you view them through binoculars, you can even track the exceedingly slow route of an individual bream as it moves through the detritus, its body angled at half-tilt while it browses on the bottom.

Whether the bream feels safer from predators at night, or whether its food is easier to gather in low light values, I am not entirely sure, but bream start to feed heavily during darkness, and with considerably more confidence than they show during the hours of daylight. Strangely, this is true of coloured and clear-water fisheries alike.

During the daylight hours of summer, stillwater bream love to browse the warm, weedy shallows and follow available food sources that drift with the wind, such as Daphnia, the largest of the freshwater zooplanktons. They porpoise on the surface when feeding at dawn and dusk, particularly during humid conditions – another useful aid to location that the angler should be well aware of (see 'Locating Bream', p. 24).

REPRODUCTION

Bream propagate their species sometime between the end of May and early July. The shoals of adult fish gather in the warm, weedy shallows, the males being quite distinct from the females by the white, knobbly spawning tubercles that are clearly visible on their heads, shoulders and pectoral fins. Old males feel rather rough over their entire body, and their tubercles never entirely fade away after spawning. Though far less pronounced than in summer, the white dots can still be seen on the fish's nose and head even during the winter months.

Prior to spawning, there is much chasing about, with the dominant males becoming noticeably aggressive. Spawning usually takes place throughout the night and ceases when the sun rises, although beneath dense patches of surface weeds where the light is diffused, odd groups could continue in fits and starts throughout much of the day.

The males usually far outnumber the females, and as they mingle among the soft weedbeds, the males continually bump into the soft flanks of the females in order to stimulate the females to release the eggs. The small, pale yellow, sticky eggs adhere to the soft weeds and are fertilized by sprays of milky white milt from the males. Where soft weeds are absent, as they are in many heavily-coloured waters, bream will use the most suitable plants available, such as the foliage of sunken tree branches or the sub-surface roots of alders and willows, reeds, rushes, sedges or lily-beds.

Depending on the water temperature, the eggs hatch within 6 to 10 days. The fry stay in their protective habitat, feeding on minute plankton in the warm shallows, until they are large enough to commence a diet of aquatic insect larvae and other bottom foods.

Hybrids

Because both roach and rudd often use the same warm, shallow spawning areas as bream, should they coincidentally arrive to complete their reproduction cycle at the same time, hybridization will occur, resulting in fish which are half-roach/half-bream or half-rudd/half-bream.

Owing to the decline of the rudd in English rivers and lakes over the past couple of decades, rudd/bream hybrids are rare. This is in complete contrast to the fisheries of southern Ireland, where rudd and bream are by far the most commonly caught species and interbreed freely to produce a spectacular hybrid. These have the bulk of the bream, growing to over 5 lb, and the distinct golden sheen of the rudd along their deep flanks. Their fins show a certain amount of warmth, but are nowhere near so red as the true rudd. These bream/rudd hybrids fight ridiculously hard and are much sought-after by visiting anglers.

Because roach (as opposed to rudd) tend to be predominant in the river systems of Northern Ireland, as they are those of England, in both countries the most common hybrid is the roach/bream. However, although the spawn and milt from both species are needed to produce a hybrid, this does not necessarily mean that the resulting fish will have exactly half the physical features of the bream and exactly half the physical features of the roach. Indeed, far from it. All kinds of shapes, colours and sizes turn up from fish that appear to be almost a true bream, yet possess the merest hint of roach ancestry, to roach that look to be a true roach, with only the slightest physical characteristics of the bream. With the roach/bream hybrid, coloration is generally grey along the back, fusing into silvery flanks covered with scales that are noticeably larger than those of the bream, yet smaller than a true roach.

The instant giveaway, however, is the hybrid's longer, decidedly bream-like anal fin, often coloured with a black band along the outside edge, and lack of red pigment in the dorsal, tail and pelvic fins. The mouth usually looks different too, with the top lip extending beyond the lower,

Because of their hard-fighting qualities bream/roach hybrids are more highly prized than the bream itself. Anglers like tackle-dealer, John Roberts, regularly make the pilgrimage over to Northern Ireland and the River Bann at Newferry, where jumbo hybrids between 2½ and 3½ lb are commonplace.

whereas in the true roach the lips are virtually level in a vertical line. In England roach/bream or bream/roach (take your pick) hybrids do not occur everywhere, the most likely areas being large, coloured, shallow stillwaters where the water warms quickly: lakes, pits, meres and broads. Hybrids are, in fact, particularly common within my local Norfolk Broads system of interconnecting lakes and tidal rivers. In certain areas they are numerous in the 1–1¾ lb class, with odd fish topping 2½ lb.

The most prolific spot I have ever fished for roach/bream hybrids is the mighty River Bann in Northern Ireland, where, in parts of the lower reaches, such as Newferry and Portglenone, they are the most commonly caught species. Fish of 2–2½ lb are commonplace, and there are large concentrations of real jumbo-hybrids running between 3 and 4 lb, which actually make up far larger-bag catches than either roach or bream. This could very well have something to do with the migration routes taken by these hybrids into the River Bann from their summer haunts in Lough Beg, a huge shallow water where massive shoals of both bream and roach congregate for spawning during the late spring or early summer every year.

From fast-flowing rivers like the Hampshire Avon, to man-made gravel pits where anglers must share the water with other users, bream provide wonderful sport.

Silver bream

Before finishing with the bream's reproductive cycle, I think a few words about the so-called silver bream are in order. Once said to be common all over East Anglia, this species, also said to reach little more than 1½ lb in weight, is so elusive that for quite some time now I have wondered whether it ever existed, or was it not all along a roach/ bream hybrid. After all, it is possible to catch a whole netful of hybrids from the same spawning that, although similar to each other, look as if they could be a different species of bream. As yet, after close on 40 years of serious freshwater fishing, I cannot ever recall seeing a worthwhile colour photograph of what purported to be a silver bream in any reference book.

I must admit, however, that when in my teens I fished the Old Bedford River at Mepal in Cambridgeshire, I regularly caught a fish that might have been a silver bream, on float-fished stewed wheat from among the thick weeds of this narrow drain. It had a larger eye than a bream of identical size, was covered in far less slime, had warmer fins, and a definite darker, outer edge to its anal and tail fins – all the hallmarks that textbooks attribute to the enigmatic silver bream. The only point that continues to worry me is that those fish might have been hybrids, because hybrids have identical characteristics.

DISTRIBUTION

Bream are found in every type of water throughout the British Isles, except in the north of Scotland. They are also found throughout the whole of Europe and much of Asia. Several species similar to the bream, including the Zope and the Danubian bream, also occur in European waters.

Although past angling literature suggested that the bream is more suited to slow-running rivers and stillwaters, it has been my experience that bream fare very well indeed in fast-flowing rivers and even in quite shallow streams. They certainly exist in far greater numbers in stillwaters, lakes, pits, meres, broads, reservoirs and in slow-moving rivers, probably due to a higher fry survival-rate, but bream nevertheless grow to a good average size in fast water, and they especially love weir-pools. Indeed, to catch them from deep, swirling waters provides the most thrilling of scraps, particularly when they turn their deep flanks side-on to the flow.

CHAPTER THREE

LOCATING BREAM

STILLWATERS

It has long been believed that bream always prefer the slowest, deepest water – during the summer at least – but nothing could be further from the truth. Even stillwater bream with a varied choice of shallow and deep areas sometimes select the warm, weedy shallows in which to spend their days. There are at least two good reasons for this. Shallow water warms up quickly and provides the bream with a protective habitat of aquatic vegetation, lilies, ribbon-weed and the like. Secondly, the amount of natural food per square foot of water is far greater in warm, shallow areas than in deeper, colder areas, and the food multiplies more rapidly.

In most really deep parts of reservoirs and gravel pits – in depths of 20 ft or more – the amount of natural food on the bottom is minimal by comparison with shallow water. Scuba-diving in many of the mature pits along my local River Wensum valley, I have seen how barren the bottom structure can be in excessive depths, with nothing on the floor except a thick, often sterile, layer of sediment.

Unless the water is crystal clear below depths of 15 ft, insufficient sunlight penetrates to stimulate bottom-rooted plant growth. The only readily available food source in excessive depths is the bloodworm (the larvae of the midge) which 'layer' in the thick deposits of accumulated silts, even where the level of dissolved oxygen is at its very lowest. This lack of oxygen becomes more pronounced during the summer months, once the water temperature starts to increase. In fact, baits presented for any length of time on the bottom in deep water often come back smelling putrid, proving the lack of dissolved oxygen in that bottom band of water. This is the reason why large shoals of bream can sometimes be seen 'layering' above the

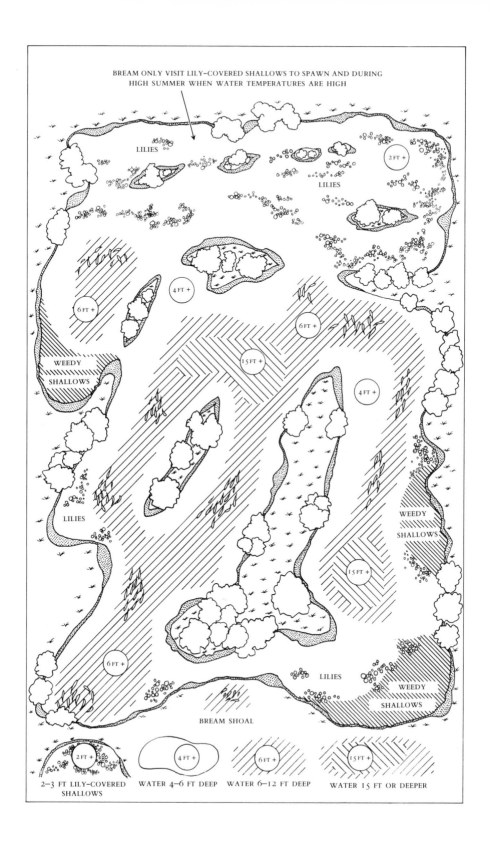

BREAM ONLY VISIT LILY–COVERED SHALLOWS TO SPAWN AND DURING HIGH SUMMER WHEN WATER TEMPERATURES ARE HIGH

LILIES

2 FT +

LILIES

4 FT +

6 FT +

6 FT +

15 FT +

4 FT +

WEEDY SHALLOWS

LILIES

WEEDY SHALLOWS

15 FT +

6 FT +

LILIES

WEEDY SHALLOWS

BREAM SHOAL

2 FT +

2–3 FT LILY–COVERED SHALLOWS

4 FT +

WATER 4–6 FT DEEP

6 FT +

WATER 6–12 FT DEEP

15 FT +

WATER 15 FT OR DEEPER

very deep water during the daylight hours, anywhere from a few feet off bottom to within inches of the surface.

FIGURE 1 *Extensive gravel pit showing prime bream locations*

However, as the bottom starts to shelve upwards from 12 to 10 to 8 ft, and then to 6 ft of water, the character of the water changes dramatically from that at the bottom. It is within this depth band – at about 6 to 12 feet – that I would expect to find most bream shoals throughout most of the season. Fig. 1 illustrates a typical gravel-pit bream habitat, and shows where the shoals are most likely to be – in areas with beds of soft weeds and lilies full of food items, colonies of freshwater mussels, a veritable mountain of aquatic insects at various stages of their life cycles, plus shrimps, asellus, snails, leeches, water-boatmen, annelid worms and many more. They are all eeking a living from the bottom detritus – that rich layer of broken-down plant cells and leaves derived from both aquatic vegetation and overhanging grasses and trees. It is small wonder that fish prefer water shallower than 15 ft whenever they have the option.

In many stillwaters, estate lakes, meres, and well-established gravel-pit fisheries, the deep and shallow areas become obvious during the summer months because of surface plant growth, such as lilies. During the winter months, however, it is a different situation.

Although in the majority of stillwaters bream will keep

FIGURE 2 *River
bream locations*

off the bottom in very deep areas (there are, of course, always exceptions), the one generalization I would make is that, taken on a calendar basis, the deeper areas are more likely to attract bream – because it is a large-bodied shoal fish – than the extreme shallows. However, depth by itself does not guarantee a good bream swim.

Bream in even-depthed stillwaters, such as meres, estate lakes, and to a large extent the Norfolk Broads (which are rather short of obvious holding-areas), can usually be located by visual signs during the months of summer and autumn. Again, dusk and dawn are the prime times to be present with binoculars at the ready, looking for patches of bubbles or the backs of bream as they porpoise. Sometimes the shoals frequent lily-beds, sometimes they are alongside dense reed-beds, so keep the binoculars handy at all times for spotting those tell-tale signs.

When the wind and sub-surface tow push vast clouds of natural food like daphnia and other zooplanktons into a particular bay, or up against a certain shoreline, the bream will feed in that area until the wind changes. At night they can be attracted to almost any spot by regular pre-baiting (see 'Pre-baiting', p. 73–5), with the most consistent results coming from areas on the shoal's natural feeding route.

On many of the Norfolk Broads, for instance, especially those connected to the tidal rivers Bure and Thurne, bream that meander through the shallow broads during the day are renowned for migrating into the river during darkness, once the boat traffic has ceased. Thus wide, junction swims at the river entrances, where the water is usually deeper owing to the continual passing of river traffic, are obvious hot-spots because the bream will at some time (usually at dusk, and again at dawn) pass through.

Sections of tidal river between broads are obvious busy areas. Deep Dyke, the junction connecting famous Hickling Broad to Heigham Sound, for instance, is hopeless for bream during daylight hours – there are none there. Only under the cloak of darkness, once the armada of holiday cruisers are tied up for the night and the sediment in the turbid waters of Deep Dyke settles, do the bream migrate from one broad to another.

Pre-baiting, of course, holds the fish, and usually keeps a proportion feeding earnestly until the dawn chorus. However, bream bites cease instantly as the first cruiser of

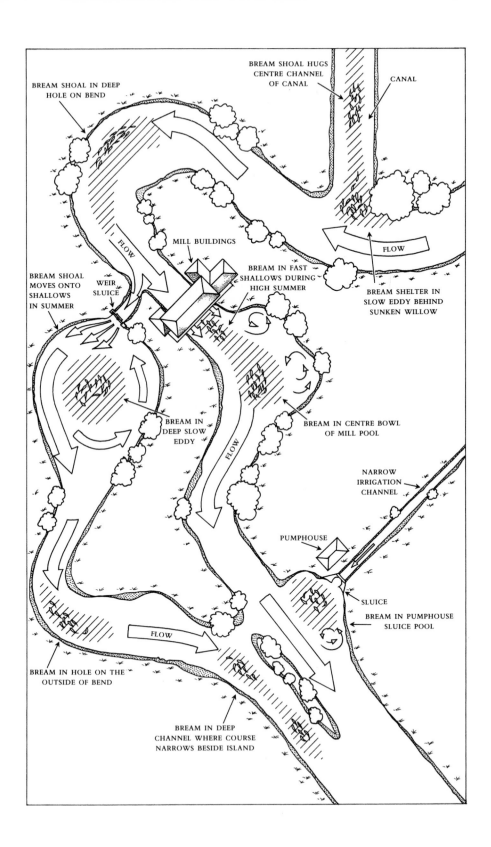

BREAM SHOAL IN DEEP
HOLE ON BEND

BREAM SHOAL HUGS
CENTRE CHANNEL
OF CANAL

CANAL

FLOW

FLOW

MILL BUILDINGS

WEIR
SLUICE

BREAM SHOAL
MOVES ONTO
SHALLOWS
IN SUMMER

BREAM IN FAST
SHALLOWS DURING
HIGH SUMMER

BREAM SHELTER IN
SLOW EDDY BEHIND
SUNKEN WILLOW

BREAM IN
DEEP SLOW
EDDY

BREAM IN CENTRE BOWL
OF MILL POOL

FLOW

NARROW
IRRIGATION
CHANNEL

PUMPHOUSE

SLUICE

BREAM IN PUMPHOUSE
SLUICE POOL

FLOW

BREAM IN HOLE ON THE
OUTSIDE OF BEND

BREAM IN DEEP
CHANNEL WHERE COURSE
NARROWS BESIDE ISLAND

Deep holes on the outside of wide bends are the favourite lies of river bream. When the river is in full spate during the winter months, however, the shoal will move across and pack tightly, close in to the bank on the inside of the bend, exactly where the angler is situated here.

the day chugs through. Many an unsuspecting holiday fisherman can be seen fishing on well into the day, completely mystified by the lack of action, and completely oblivious to the fact that the shoal his bait lay among only an hour earlier is now more than half a mile away.

RIVERS

In rivers, where the water is continually on the move, thus oxygenating the bottom strata, bream can be expected in the deepest areas, where they will be feeding on shrimps, snails and aquatic insect larvae, at all times of the year except the spring, when they vacate the deeps for shallow spawning areas (fig. 2). In the mighty River Shannon in southern Ireland, for instance, where depths range from 15 to 25 ft, bream abound in massive shoals only two or three rod-lengths out from the bank. Strangely, and like bream everywhere, there are always a few that pop up to the surface at dusk and dawn (and throughout the night),

rolling tantalizingly and giving away the shoal's exact position. These rolling bream are either responding to the joy of life or sucking in aquatic flies as they are about to hatch. They can even be seen lunging into concentrations of young fry massed in the warmer, upper water layers.

When bream appear at the surface on a deep-water river, it could be that the shoal is layered throughout 20 ft of water, with the occasional fish at the top of the shoal sticking its head out and porpoising; or it could be that the shoal is hugging the bottom, with the occasional fish suddenly deciding to swim upwards 20 ft to break surface. I would suggest that in most cases it is the former rather than the latter, having witnessed this layering and por-poising on numerous occasions when bream fishing the gin-clear waters of my local Norfolk rivers, the Wensum and the Upper Waveney, during the summer months. In such waters, the antics of the entire shoal can be observed. Initially the shoal has been layered, with those on top most likely to break surface and roll. Once loose feed or groundbait is located by the lower fish, encouraging them to get their heads down, those occupying the upper

All weir-pool complexes provide great attraction to river bream during the summer months due to the high levels of dissolved oxygen in the fast, bubbly water. This massive weir spans the River Shannon in southern Ireland, where bream between 4 and 7 lb are commonplace.

layers quickly follow suit. This results in instant bites,
sometimes within only a few seconds of the bait settling on
the bottom.

This seemingly wonderful state of affairs, however,
with ever member of the shoal feeding with gay abandon,
is not necessarily desirable, because false bites can result.
Being exceptionally deep-bodied with large fins, and
feeding in close proximity to each other, feeding fish
cannot always avoid your line; and although the indicator
registers a genuine bite, the line has simply caught around
the bream's fins. If, when ledgering, you repeatedly strike
without connecting to a fish, this usually indicates a
preponderance of line bites. This problem is more common
in stillwaters than flowing water (see 'Line Bites', p. 124),
and occurs most frequently in really shallow fisheries of
between 2 and 5 ft in depth.

Fortunately, line bites are rarely a problem when seeking
the noticeably darker-coloured bream of fast, clear-
flowing, shallow and weedy rivers. Such rivers offer a
fascinating proposition and a completely different challenge
from their stillwater counterparts.

Indeed, some rivers would appear to flow with far too
much pace to contain this supposedly sluggish species. A
river like the Hampshire Avon, for instance, best known
for its salmon, seatrout and barbel, in fact contains a
fabulous head of bream in its lower reaches. It is possible in
most swims to locate the shoals of bream visually, just like
the barbel and chub. By peering into the fast, smooth
water through polaroid sunglasses, you can observe
relatively large shoals of up to sixty or eighty bream
packed close together in quite narrow runs between the
long, flowing beds of rununculus and potomogeton.

The famous Royalty Fishery in Christchurch holds
terrific concentrations of hard-battling bream with barely a
trace of slime on their firm, golden-bronze bodies, and it is
not difficult to locate them visually from June through to
October. I have good reason for valuing the bream in the
Avon, because it was on the tidal reaches of the Royalty
Fishery in 1989 that *Angling Times* arranged the last of
three matches between England team manager, Dick
Clegg, and myself. Billed as a modern-day re-run of the
'original' Dick Walker–Tom Sails match held 35 years
previously, with the emphasis on the specimen hunter or

big-fish man versus the matchman, the Avon contest – the final leg after poor results on the Rivers Witham and Bain – was always going to be won with either chub or bream. For that reason, the evening before the match, once everyone had finished dinner and the pre-match chat was over, I went to my room and soaked two old loaves in the wash-basin. I planned to use mashed bread groundbait, just in case I was fortunate enough to draw a swim containing bream.

As luck would have it, this is exactly what happened. Dick won the toss and chose the best-looking swim on the stretch, immediately below the motorway road-bridge, where the tidal Avon splits around a long island. This was a classic, tree-lined chub swim that, on the day, did not produce. I settled for a long, wide, shallow run split down the middle by an extremely shallow gravel bar that was only inches deep at the bottom of the tide. It was not in any way a classic bream swim, but it turned out to hold bream nonetheless.

Despite a particularly raw day, and with no more than 3 ft of water covering their backs, those bream moved on to the carpet of mashed bread and continued to feed with enough confidence for me to be able to bustle nine fish of up to 5 lb away from the shoal during the last 2½ hours of the 4-hour contest.

All came to quivertipped breadflake on a three-swan-shot fixed paternoster ledger and gave characteristic, extremely gentle, drop-back bites. This type of bite is a hallmark of fast-water bream. They cannot always turn completely around with the bait and move to the back of the shoal when they are so tightly grouped in such a small area, and are hemmed in front and back and on either side by other shoal members.

By turning their deep bodies side-on to the strong flow, those bream produced a surprising level of resistance, against which it was all I could do to pump them 30 yd upstream to where I sat. The biggest, a whopper of fully 8 lb if it was an ounce, I lost by pulling the hook from its top lip in my impatience to see it inside the landing-net before it was ready. Nevertheless, the nine bream and a lone chub that did end up in the net totalled 35 lb, winning me the match. Far more important, however – Dick Clegg and I have been firm friends ever since.

It may be difficult to believe, but anglers tackling the fast waters of the famous Royalty Fishery on the Hampshire Avon shown here above the motorway bridge in Christchurch, can expect quality bream in real numbers in addition to salmon, seatrout, chub and barbel.

The 100 yard stretch immediately below the same bridge was the scene of in 1989 a match between England Team Manager Dick Clegg and the author, staged by Angling Times. Both anglers caught chub to over 4 lb as expected, but John proved the pulling power of breadflake, ledgered over a carpet of mashed bread, with a catch of nine deep-bodied winter bream from a fast swim just 3 ft deep.

WEIR-POOLS

As mentioned earlier, bream are attracted to the fast, swirling waters of weir-pools, both deep and shallow. During the hottest part of the year, when the water table is low and levels of dissolved oxygen throughout the entire river are correspondingly low, bream congregate in weir-pools, and even occupy the fastest runs. Being of slim profile when viewed head-on, they can in fact happily hold station against considerably faster currents than you would expect. So search for the shoals through polaroid glasses (even in turbulent water) from midday onwards when the sun is at its highest to pinpoint their exact location. The occasional rolling bream can be expected at dusk or dawn in the slower parts of the pool during summer and autumn, but in general fast-water bream tend not to porpoise with anywhere near the same regularity as those inhabiting slow-moving rivers and stillwaters.

Once winter sets in, do not expect any visual pointers,

Many bream anglers are naturally deterred by the fast currents of weir pools. Yet when water levels are low, there is no more pleasurable way of catching summer bream than dragging the bait slowly along the bottom of a deep, slow eddy beneath a waggler float.

even from resident weir-pool bream. They will be down on the bottom in a deepish, comfortable part of the pool where the flow is slowest. Careful use of the plummet and a sliding-float rig will determine the most likely holding-spots. Or tie a small bomb to the end of your line and count it down to the bottom to achieve the same results and acquire a quick outline of the pool's deeps and shallows. Do not, however, be led into thinking that the deepest water always exists where the surface current is slowest. Depending on which sluices are open, and in which direction the flow is channelled, the surface might be fast and turbulent, but those last few feet immediately above the bottom of large depressions could be slow-moving and much to the liking of a bream shoal (see 'Quivertipping', p. 108).

The most fabulous weir-pool bream fishing I have ever experienced was at Meelick on the River Shannon in southern Ireland, where a narrow catwalk spans the entire weir sill across the river, which at this point is 200 yd wide. This unique balustrade provides easy access to any part of the weir, regardless of water levels or which sluices are open.

While filming a *Go Fishing* TV programme at Meelick, I decided to try one of the deep pools that are usually very turbulent. Bream would be the last species expected; the spot is, in fact, a favourite salmon run. Yet on this occasion in September, when water levels were extremely low, the main pool was absolutely packed with bream that had moved up from the lower reaches, attracted by the increased levels of dissolved oxygen.

I was joined on the weir sill by friends Ray Bows and Malcolm Butler from Sheffield, and in the space of only a few hours we amassed an enormous haul of bream to over 7 lb, plus a sprinkling of small perch and those beautiful rudd/bream hybrids ranging between 2 and 3 lb. All came to simple waggler floatfishing tactics: a bunch of five maggots on a size 10 hook cast slightly over-depth to the opposite side of the large, slow eddy, and the float allowed to come around slowly with the flow.

Initially we introduced a few balls of cereal groundbait laced with maggot and caster, followed thereafter by the occasional handful of loose feed dropped into the flush. This was enough to keep the bream active, and our

combined haul must have totalled well over 400 lb. Ray
Bows alone took an estimated 200 lb, and all from a weir-
pool eddy most anglers would have ignored as a bream
hot-spot.

CANALS AND THE FENS

In narrow, slow-moving rivers that are similar throughout
their length – such as canals or the drains of Cambridgeshire
and Lincolnshire, for instance, which have shallow
marginal edges along both banks dropping slowly away to
a deeper, uniform centre channel – bream will predictably
choose to occupy the area down the middle. During the
summer months, the shoals are nomadic and browse like
cattle. They often travel great distances in the course of a
day, feeding from the thick, rich layer of organic silt that
accumulates on the bottom of the central bowl.

Regardless of whether bream are porpoising on the
surface or not, with the aid of binoculars you should be
able to determine the existence of feeding shoals by paying
attention to the colour of the water. Hundreds of adult
bream rooting through the bottom detritus noticeably
colours a large area, and once your eyes have learnt to
distinguish these patches of discoloured water, you will
also notice numerous clusters of tiny feeding bubbles
littering the surface film.

On summer club outings to the Cambridgeshire Fens
when I was a teenager, I quickly discovered that finding
patches of coloured water was the key to coming among the
prize money. In those days, club matches were 'rovers';
everyone picked a number from the hat, and once all were
taken they walked off to a swim of their own choice. The
angler unlucky enough to pick number 40 (there were
usually 40 on the coach) held the hat out and asked number 1
to go. After a few seconds number 2 put his token in the hat
and also walked off to wherever he fancied, and so on. It was
a far easier and far less time-consuming method than
'pegging down' the stretch to be fished (there was of course
far less pressure on waters in those days from both anglers
and agriculture), and the only rule was that you did not

With a thick carpet of overnight snow covering the canal towpath, Kevin Ashurst has not picked the best conditions for locating bream. Yet he did eventually get among them in the late afternoon by offering a single red maggot just tripping bottom through the deep centre channel immediately below the pole tip.

overtake the lower number in front until he had put his tackle down at his chosen swim.

The most worthwhile aspect of this system was that it allowed the individual to use his watercraft to select the most likely spot, instead of having to sit all day at a useless peg. But that's by-the-by. Rover fishing taught me to wait until I located visible signs of bream, and on the drains of Cambridgeshire I always looked for discoloured water or fish topping. At one particular venue where two drains ran almost side by side for mile upon mile, with just a high flood bank between them, it was possible (again with the aid of binoculars) by walking slowly along the top of the bank to reconnoitre both drains simultaneously for patches of discoloured water or the sight of rolling bream.

When fishing these drains independently, I could arrive at dawn. This made location easy because of the sheer numbers of bream topping, as they do in the early morning mist. (Club outings, however, were rather long-winded affairs, and very rarely did the coach arrive at the water before the sun was well up with most signs of rolling bream long gone.) In feature areas where the surface had become clogged with lilies, bream were naturally expected, being attracted to the surface shade like flies to a honey-pot. Sometimes, however, the entire surface of the drain might be covered with lilies from bank to bank and for mile upon mile. Obviously bream could not be every-where. Even then, however, it was usually possible to pinpoint a few shoals by observing sections of the lily-pads through binoculars.

It is virtually impossible for hundreds of fish to move about down below without one occasionally brushing against and moving the vertical stems of the lilies, and areas of the water where several pads could be seen 'twitching' or 'swaying' at the same time (accompanied by the odd cluster of bubbles rising to the surface), contained the largest bream concentrations.

It was a far better method of location than groundbaiting a picturesque spot, or a swim that was either comfortable or easy to fish, and waiting for a shoal to pass by.

Night fishing usually proves rewarding to a 'baiting-and-waiting routine', because wherever they live bream naturally feed with more aggression during darkness. However, when the air temperature drops rapidly during the early hours beneath clear skies, shrouding the surface in a thick mist, inevitably a lull in feeding activity will occur, followed by a resurgence and much porpoising as dawn breaks. It is as if the bream has been given the job of heralding in the start of a new day.

CHAPTER FOUR

TACKLE

BECAUSE adult bream are likely to succumb to almost any offering, from a single maggot dangling on a size 24 hook to a giant, hard-baked boilie presented on a shock rig intended for carp, there is no standardized bream tackle. Specialized bream rods, for instance, are not available. Indeed, what makes the bream so appealing is the fact that it may be caught with a whole variety of tackle combinations and methods geared to the size of fish expected. Remember always to fish, if anything, on the lighter side rather than the heavier so that the fish's fight can be fully enjoyed.

Only light float tackle and a fine-tipped match rod (or pole set-up), for instance, will permit maximum enjoyment to be obtained from skimmer bream averaging just a few ounces apiece living in the almost static water of a canal. Whereas to control specimens of 5 and 6 lb plus, hooked in the fast currents of the River Severn or Hampshire Avon, a $1\frac{1}{4}$-lb test curve, Avon-actioned ledger rod coupled to a 5 lb reel line would in no way prove over powerful.

RODS

Float rods

To cover most situations in bream fishing, both float and ledger rods are required. For accurate presentation of the bait in certain conditions and locations, a telescopic or take-apart pole is an indispensible tool.

Let us start with the float rod. Thirteen foot is an ideal length, although for regular fishing with a fixed float at long range or into deep water, a 14-footer will prove a better choice because it picks up more line on the strike. A lightweight, three-piece, carbon-fibre, waggler-style match rod – snappy on the strike yet with a cushioning, forgiving action for use with small hooks and taking into account the bream's soft mouth tissue – is absolutely perfect, permitting the use of reel lines of 2–4 lb test and, when necessary, hook lengths down to 1 lb test.

Poles

For reaching out over a bream shoal and presenting the float directly beneath the tip at distances up to 10–12 yd in slow-moving and still water, there is nothing to match the effectiveness of the pole. When bream are no more than a few yards out, staying in one place and feeding confidently either because of heavily coloured water or because they are shielded from the angler by a thick marginal covering of surface plants, such as lilies, opt for an inexpensive, lightweight telescopic pole of 5–6 m incorporating a solid glass 'flick-tip'. These poles, which at lengths of 18–20 ft are easily held like a rod, supported by the forearm, bend nicely in the tip section and easily subdue even large bream with little chance of a 2–3 lb test line parting when tied direct to the small end-ring.

When presenting the bait to bream situated further out, at distances of about 25–40 ft, a 10–12 m lightweight, reinforced-carbon pole is *the* tool to use. Generally speaking, you get what you pay for, and top-quality poles are considerably lighter and more rigid than budget-priced models. Poles manufactured by Shimano, Daiwa and Browning are particularly recommended, and you have the option of tying the line directly to the flick-tip, or dispensing with the tip altogether by cutting it back carefully with a fine-tooth hacksaw, and adding a PTFE bush, through which runs high-stretch pole elastic (see 'Pole Fishing', p. 93).

Ledger/quivertip rods

Match fishing has created a demand for many different types of rods, and the range of swingtip, quivertip and standard ledger rods currently available to suit various ledgering requirements is staggering. It is imperative, therefore, to purchase the correct rod for the job at hand.

A 13-ft waggler-style rod is without question the most versatile floatfishing tool, whether presenting the lift method just beyond the marginal shelf, or casting a heavier slider rig way out to the bream inhabiting an Irish lough.

For close- to medium-range ledgering in stillwaters and slow-moving rivers, an easy-actioned, carbon-fibre, two-piece, 9–10 footer fitted with a threaded tip-ring is ideal. It can be used in conjunction with a bobbin bite-indicator clipped on between reel and butt-ring, or with either a swingtip or a quivertip screwed into the tip-ring (see 'Bite Indicators', p. 52–3).

Alternatively, and very much nicer to use, is a 10–11 ft rod with a built-in quivertip, again in lightweight carbon fibre. A rod with a soft-actioned tip is the best all-round choice for registering the often delicate bites of the bream. If, however, you only ever fish deep, fast-flowing rivers, choose a fairly rigid 11–12 footer with a medium quivertip.

If you want a rod capable of dealing with bream living in any type of environment, there are two choices. The 10–11 ft carbon-fibre, multi-tip quiver is, without question, the most versatile tool, and comes with a choice of three or four tapered tips of varying strengths (stored in the rod's handle). It is suitable for bream in both still and fast-flowing waters. Alternatively (for those whose fishing leans towards specimen-sized bream – say, of 5 lb and

upwards), the 11–12 ft, 1¼ lb test curve, carbon, Avon twin-tip ledger rod is the best choice. It incorporates both standard (with a threaded end-ring) and finely-tapered quivertip tops, and will handle just about every situation demanded by larger-than-average bream, from bobbin fishing at distance in large stillwaters to quivertipping in fast, deep waters. Lightweight, specialist, carbon-fibre ledger rods manufactured by Ryobi, Daiwa and Shakespeare are particularly recommended.

For all close-range work, from the incredibly deep marginal drop-offs in gravel pits to the centre channel of a canal, the pole permits the most natural bait presentation and use of the lightest terminal rigs for shy, clear-water bream.

REELS

Centre-pin reels

Because of the way in which the thumb immediately releases the drum, enabling line to be given instantly and so minimizing pressure on fine lines and small hooks, the centre-pin is unquestionably the best reel when floatfishing for bream at close range. I have two favourites in regular use – the time-proven Match Aerial and an Adcock

Stanton. However, because its casting range is limited, the centre-pin is not practical for any other bream-fishing situations.

Fixed-spool reels

The ideal reel is a small-format, lightweight, fixed-spool that incorporates a roller in the bale arm. I prefer those that run smoothly on ball-bearings, and which also possess a super-sensitive, slipping clutch. Small hooks are pulled from the bream's soft mouth-tissue all too often if the reel's drag has not been correctly adjusted, or is not sensitive enough. Ideally, the reel should come with an extra spool, providing you with a choice of, say, 2–2½ lb test for float work and 3½–5 lb for ledgering. Reels whose spools have been designed to take just 100 yd of either test without the need for unwanted backing line are particularly recommended.

There is no point in wasting money on 300 yd of 2 lb line when seeking a fish which, even when specimen sized, is rarely going to pull more than a few yards off on the run.

Reel manufacturers such as Shimano, Daiwa and Ryobi offer a range of varying models in sizes from 1000 upwards. My choice is for the 2000 to 2500 size; no larger. It is usually the case that larger-format reels are less complementary to fine lines and can therefore reduce the enjoyment of catching small fish. The ardent match angler, however, would perhaps prefer the extra speed provided by reels with automatic bale arms, where the cast is made with the forefinger of the rod-hand by depressing the bale arm – reels such as the famous Mitchell Match, which has a front-adjusting clutch, and Ryobi's stern-drag Master Match 300.

Only when ledgering at long range – say 60 yd plus – for specimen bream, when lines of 6 lb test are necessary and a narrow-spooled reel would greatly limit both the cast and the retrieve, do I change to a larger format. Much of my bream fishing over the past 20 years has been done with the (now unobtainable) Baby Mitchell 308 (also called the 'prince') because of its super-sensitive clutch. I think it a great shame that a large proportion of today's anglers insist on playing fish by backwinding rather than with the slipping clutch. The majority of good-quality, small-format, stern-drag reels now on the market possess extremely smooth, slipping clutch mechanisms, and learning to use the drag knob so that line is taken only at a certain pressure is a most fulfilling and enjoyable part of playing the fish. And, once mastered, it will stand you in good stead wherever you seek bream.

LINES

A selection of reel lines between 2 lb and 5 lb test will cover all bream-fishing requirements, except for long-range ledgering. This will require a step up to 6 lb test, which provides a sensible safety margin for the continual casting of heavy bombs or swimfeeders. Brands that I have used exhaustively over the years and recommend for their reliability are Sylcast, Bayer Perlon and Maxima.

For floatfishing I carry spools loaded with 2, 3 and 4 lb, while the rigours of ledgering demand strengths of 4, 5 and 6 lb test. A few spools of lighter hook-length material – say, 12 oz, $1\frac{1}{4}$ lb and $1\frac{3}{4}$ lb test – will also be required for the delicate presentation of casters or maggots on tiny hooks. Being much finer in diameter than standard monofilament, low-stretch brands such as Aikens 'Concept 2000' and Drennan 'Double Strength' make excellent hook lengths. Do not, however, be tempted into choosing low-stretch monofilament for the reel. The elasticity, or 'stretch', in standard monofilament is your buffer and safeguard against ripping out small hooks, or even snapping up, when playing a big fish too hard. When pole-fishing, however, a length of low-stretch mono is perfectly in order because the elastic provides the buffer.

HOOKS

Bream fishing demands that you carry a comprehensive selection of hooks, from fine-wire size 22 spade-ends up to size 6 forged eyes. The dividing line when choosing spade-ends against eyed hooks occurs for me at around size 14. In

Avon-style, built-in quivertip ledger rods (note the matt-white tip for maximum visibility) combine sensitive bite indication from the shyest bream, with enough power to extract specimens from the deepest rivers.

the smaller sizes, for presenting baits such as maggots, I opt for spade-ends because they appear neater and are available in a variety of wire strengths to suit that of the hook length. For use with a 12-oz bottom for instance, fine-wire, micro-barb patterns like the Kamasan B520 are ideal, whereas for tying direct to a 2 lb reel line, a forged pattern such as the Kamasan B640 is advisable.

From size 14 up to size 6, I used eyed hooks exclusively. The Drennan chemically-etched, round-bend, straight-eyed, carbon specimen hook is perfect for all baits, from particles such as sweetcorn to a large lobworm or lump of bread flake.

KNOTS

I use two knots for tying on eyed hooks (fig. 3). With large hooks, where the line can be passed twice through the eye, there is nothing to beat the mahseer knot (fig. 3A). However, the eye of smaller-sized, chemically-etched eyed hooks is invariably so neat that this knot is not possible, so use the seven-turn, 'tucked' half blood knot (fig. 3B) instead.

Fixed-spool reels in the 2000–2500 size with the capacity of up to 100 yd of 5 lb test will cope with the hardest fighting bream, like this 6-pounder extracted from a deep weir-pool by TV film director, Paul Martingell.

When tying spade-end hooks to the finest monofilament, the knot must be both strong and neat. Excellent tools, such as the 'Matchman Hook-Tyer', exist for those whose fingers or eyes won't co-operate. Or you can attempt the simple spade-end knot shown in fig. 3C, which requires no threading or special tool, and permits the smallest of hooks to be tied neatly and quickly.

For joining a fine hook-link to the reel line, or for constructing a simple fixed-paternoster ledger rig, consider the four-turn water knot in fig. 4A. This reliable knot allows you to add a thicker ledger-link (to alleviate tangles) to a lighter reel line (fig. 4B), or to join a fine hook-link to the reel line when bream are biting extra shyly (fig. 4C).

Running ledger rigs play no part in my bream fishing whatsoever. I consider them unnecessary and an over-complication of the end tackle. Simple rigs are the key to confidence and to finishing with fish in the net, quite apart from the fact that one tiny knot junction creates minimal resistance and picks up nowhere near so much weed as swivels, beads, booms and so-called anti-tangle devices.

FIGURE 3 *Knots 1*

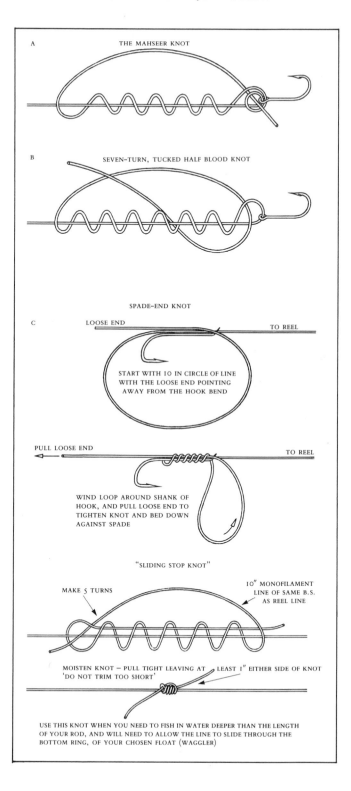

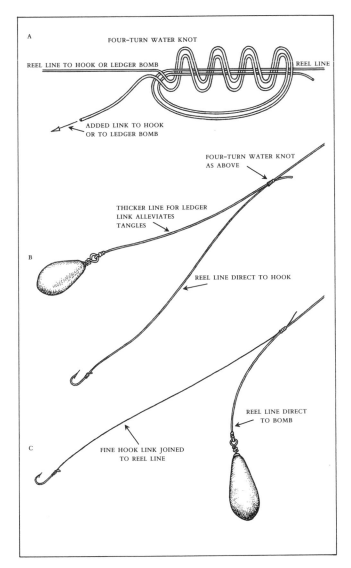

A
FOUR-TURN WATER KNOT
REEL LINE TO HOOK OR LEDGER BOMB   REEL LINE
ADDED LINK TO HOOK
OR TO LEDGER BOMB

FOUR-TURN WATER KNOT
AS ABOVE

THICKER LINE FOR LEDGER
LINK ALLEVIATES
TANGLES

B

REEL LINE DIRECT TO HOOK

REEL LINE DIRECT
TO BOMB

C

FINE HOOK LINK JOINED
TO REEL LINE

FIGURE 4 *Knots 2*

FLOATS

Though river bream can be caught close in by trotting
with a stick float, these occasions are quite rare. For both
still and flowing water, waggler-style or bottom-end-only
floats are recommended, enabling the bait to be presented
naturally – either static on the bottom, or trundling along
slowly, or moving just off the bottom at current pace.

A point worth remembering is that of all species, bream

The popular 'long pole-short line' technique allows Ian Heaps to trot his bait slowly along, just tripping bottom through the deeper centre channel of this narrow, enchanting river. The pole tip has been fitted with an elastic 'internal conversion', permitting the use of extremely small hooks and gossamer-thin lines.

are the least likely to chase the bait. For the lift method, and for standard waggler presentations, I regularly use both straight and tipped (insert) peacock wagglers, in sizes from two BB to giant stems carrying 2½ swan shots.

The extra carrying capacity and consequent greater stability of bodied peacock wagglers makes them extremely useful for distant swims; and they keep the bait static in lakes and pits affected by strong winds and sub-surface tow. A range carrying from two AA up to 3½ swan shots should suffice. On the lighter side, a slim-tipped range of 'stillwater greens', or similar antennas, varying from two No. 1 to five BB is most useful for shy-biting bream and for exact presentation when fishing close in or on a flat-calm surface.

Pole floats

While the collecting of pole floats and ready-made rigs on winders is to many almost a hobby in itself, I will stick my neck out and say that you can easily cope with most situations when bream fishing by using just two float types. A range of oval-bodied, wire stem, bristle-top floats with a shotting capacity from 0.20 grams up to, say, 1 gram will do nicely for stillwater fishing. For flowing water a more portly set is required: heart- or round-shaped bodies carrying from 1 to 8 grams.

FIGURE 5 Pole tip elastic conversion – using standard pole elastic kit

Pole tips

There are two ways of joining your ready-made-up float rig to the pole tip: either directly, to a small ring glued on to the end of the flick-tip (some tips already have these tiny rings fitted), or by doing away with the flick-tip altogether and constructing an elastic tip.

Flick-tip fishing is best when you are using reasonably large hooks and big baits, say size 14 to size 8 tied direct to 2–5 lb line, which in turn is tied direct to the tip-ring. However, as many situations using the 'long pole/short line' set-up demand super-fine hook-lengths down to a 1 lb bottom or less, and size 18–22 hooks that all too easily tear out on a direct line, an elastic tip acting as a buffer will

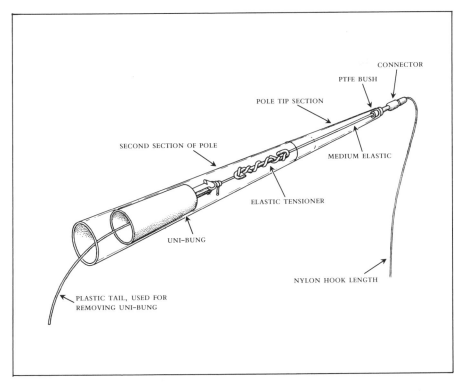

CONNECTOR

PTFE BUSH

POLE TIP SECTION

SECOND SECTION OF POLE

MEDIUM ELASTIC

ELASTIC TENSIONER

UNI–BUNG

NYLON HOOK LENGTH

PLASTIC TAIL, USED FOR
REMOVING UNI–BUNG

FIGURE 6 *Swingtip target board*

prove indispensable. It takes only a few minutes to convert the pole tip using one of the many kits available (fig. 5). You start by cutting back the tip carefully, a little at a time, so that the hollow PTFE bush fits in neatly. Use a fine-tooth hacksaw for this, and smooth the edges with fine glass paper or emery cloth. The rig connector will now fit inside the bush, but first tie on the elastic supplied with the kit and thread it down through the tip.

Into the other (wider) end of the second section, fit the coned 'uni-bung', to which the other end of the elastic is tied. The wide end of the plastic uni-bung may be reduced in diameter so that it fits neatly several inches up inside the second section, leaving the fine plastic tail protruding. To pull the bung out again for alteration to, or a complete change of, elastic you simply pull gently on the plastic tail.

Lastly, apply a few drops of elastic lubricant to the elastic to protect it against abrasion, and the tip is complete.

SWINGTIPS

To equip yourself for swingtip ledgering in stillwater, you will need a lightweight tip of between 10 and 12 in. Those constructed from fibre-glass are excellent. Ensure that the end-ring is of reasonable quality (so it will not chafe the line) and that the silicone junction is pliable without being uncontrollably sloppy. As with floats, choose one with a fluorescent coloured band on the end of the tip that you can identify and see easily.

For ledgering in very slow-moving rivers (anything faster than a slow flow becomes impractical for a swingtip and is the point at which you should switch over to the quivertip), or in stillwater whenever a strong pull or underwater tow proves troublesome and is forever slowly raising a lightweight swingtip, you will require a loaded or weighted tip.

To help you determine the slightest of bites, particularly during windy conditions, a simple target-board (you can easily make your own) placed immediately behind the swingtip will prove invaluable. It should be oblong, and screwed into an angle lock and a short, telescopic bank

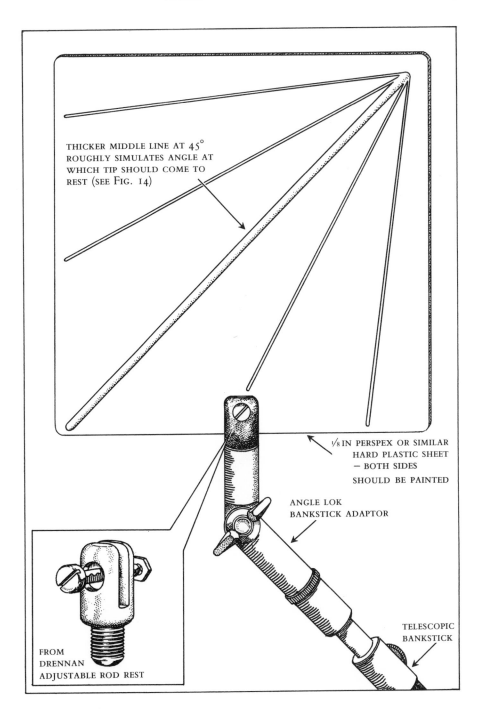

THICKER MIDDLE LINE AT 45°
ROUGHLY SIMULATES ANGLE AT
WHICH TIP SHOULD COME TO
REST (SEE FIG. 14)

⅛ IN PERSPEX OR SIMILAR
HARD PLASTIC SHEET
— BOTH SIDES
SHOULD BE PAINTED

ANGLE LOK
BANKSTICK ADAPTOR

TELESCOPIC
BANKSTICK

FROM
DRENNAN
ADJUSTABLE ROD REST

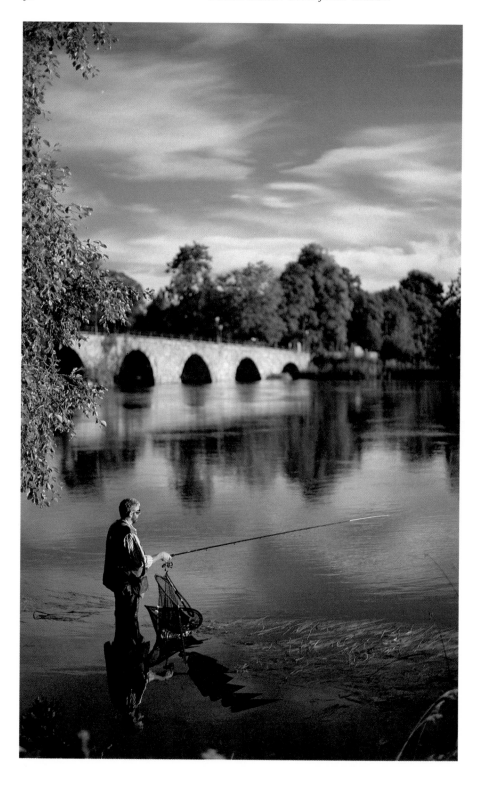

stick for exact adjustment. It can be painted in various
ways to make bites immediately apparent. A series of
angled lines starting from the top left corner on one side
and the top right corner on the reverse side, with the centre
line at an angle of 45°, is a reliable format (see fig. 6); use
either white lines on a black board or black lines on a white
board. Play around and experiment until you find a
combination to suit your personal requirements.

*Unless you select the
correct screw-in or
push-in quivertip to
match the current
strength, a percentage
of bites may never be
seen. John uses his
Avon quivertip to
present ledgered
breadflake hard on the
bottom of a deep, fast
run in Sweden's
Klaralven River.*

QUIVERTIPS

Good-quality quivertips made from carefully tapered solid
fibre-glass or carbon fibre are available in a range of test
curves to suit just about any situation from choppy
stillwater to the strongest river currents. And just like
specialist rods, they are now rated in test curves. A 1-oz
test curve quivertip, for instance, would be considered
super-sensitive, suitable for stillwater or the most gentle of
currents. One of $3\frac{1}{2}$ oz has a powerful, rapid-taper action
and is designed for use in the most powerful currents.

As for colour, it is best if the entire quivertip is painted
matt white, which shows up boldly against most backgrounds, particularly in overcast conditions when light
values are low. Most manufacturers, however, produce a
choice of various fluorescent coloured tips, so the choice is
yours.

I insist on whipping a tiny extra ring onto commercially
produced quivertips halfway between the tip-ring and the
threaded end, so that the line follows the contour of the tip
when under full compression.

A problem with some quivertips is that the tip-ring does
not line up with that of the rod once they have been
screwed in tightly. So ensure that the one you purchase is
fitted with a stiff rubber junction above the thread, which
permits the tip to be rotated for alignment.

It has been my experience as a tackle-dealer that most
anglers do not pay enough attention to the sensitivity of
quivertips, which is especially critical when ledgering for
bream. As a result, a large percentage of shy bites are not
even seen, let alone struck. So endeavour to use the finest
and most sensitive tip that conditions and current strength
will permit.

BITE INDICATORS

Bobbin indicators

When you are ledgering at distance for bream in stillwaters, a ledger bobbin clipped on to the line between the butt-ring and the reel is the ideal indicator. I use the bobbin for most stillwater ledgering. Being connected to a retaining cord, it falls to the ground when you strike and permits full enjoyment from the rod being used, as opposed to having a swingtip screwed into the tip-ring clanging about on the line.

Day-time bobbins are available in startling red or orange; or you can invest in a 'glo bobbin', which contains a luminous betalight element that lasts for 15 years. To obtain the ultimate in visibility, simply paint a band of bright red or orange at the top of a glo bobbin. It then becomes instantly visible regardless of light conditions 24 hours a day.

As a bobbin retaining cord there is nothing better than 2–3 ft of fly line (your tackle dealer should oblige for a few pence), which, being limp and low-stretch, does not make the bobbin twang back and twist around the rod-rest on the strike.

Electric bite alarms/buzzers

When ledgering through the long, dark hours from dusk until dawn, and when ledgering in lakes or pits where fish density is low and where the bream are of decidedly specimen proportions but bites are few and far between, it is comforting to use the bobbin indicator in conjunction with an electronic bite alarm for that instant, audible signal. During daylight hours, it allows you to relax and scan the surface with binoculars, to enjoy the natural history, and even to capitalize on the occasional bonus fish by instantly repositioning the bait directly over a bream should one suddenly roll well away from the area being fished.

Most of this is simply not possible, of course, if hour upon hour your eyes are gazing down at the bobbins,

daring them to move. Top of the bite alarms is the
Optonic, because it indicates both slow and fast bites in a
series of individual bleeps. It comes in several formats,
both as compact and corded units, which quickly screw
into a telescopic bank-stick and in effect become the front
rod-rest. The basic compact models without volume
control, which emit a gentle high or low bleep, are perfect
for bream fishing, as it does not demand the deafening
alarm-call so beloved by carp fishermen who have nodded
off.

SUNDRIES

Landing-nets

In fisheries where only small skimmer bream are expected,
and also when, through the necessity of club or match
fishing, speed in landing your catch is imperative, an 18–20
in triangular or round landing-net with a shallow pan-
bottom, incorporating a lightweight fibre-glass frame, will
suffice. However, as even a modest-sized bream of 3–4 lb
is a deep and relatively long fish, probably 20 in or more, a
round net with a 24-in diameter is the perfect size. My net
has 24-in deep sides in minnow-mesh, which alleviates the
possibility of a good fish accidentally jumping or rolling
out (as can happen with shallow-pan nets) plus a micro-
base for eliminating those awkward tangles that occur
when shots drop through larger meshes.

Another excellent, bream-friendly, alternative 24-in
diameter net is the Keenet standard 'safematch mix mesh'.
This has deep sides, made from a mesh slightly larger than
minnow-mesh, and a punched-hole, soft-material pan-
base called 'safe flo'. Incidentally, when weighing your
bream there is no need for a specialized weigh-sling. The
fish is already encased in the perfect receptacle and comes
to far less harm if, after removing the hook, you simply
unscrew the landing-net from its handle and hoist it
straight on to the scales, remembering to deduct the
weight of the net afterwards. Of all our freshwater species,
especially those caught during the summer months, bream
are by far the most susceptible to stress or damage through

Opposite: *When enjoying the tranquillity of huge stillwaters while playing the waiting game of long, all-night sessions in search of larger-than-average bream, opt for a two-rod set-up and bobbin bite indicators in conjunction with electronic bite alarms.*

Left: *Whether breaming in still or running water, John prefers a long, light landing-net handle for reaching out over marginal vegetation, to which is fitted a round, 23-in diameter net with a deep, micromesh bar.*

Below: *To provide a large haul of bream with the maximum protection, always use the largest keep-net available, preferably in soft, dark micromesh.*

the removal of their protective slime by excessive, uncaring handling.

As there will be times when you need to reach far out beyond thick beds of marginal sedges, reeds or lilies to net a fish, invest in a long, lightweight, telescopic pole. I use a rigid hollow-glass 10-footer. Those made from noticeably lighter, reinforced carbon-fibre are most desirable, but are extremely expensive.

Keep-nets

As I have mentioned already, bream are more susceptible to stress problems caused by being constantly handled and crammed en mass into keep-nets (often in nets which are nowhere near large enough) than all other species. During the warmest months, when oxygen levels are liable to be particularly low (and in heavily-coloured, shallow still-waters especially, dissolved oxygen levels can be danger-ously low), the sensible approach is not to retain your catch. Provide them with the best possible chance of recovery by returning them to the water immediately, remembering to wet your hands fully before removing the hook and taking the bream from the net. It takes but a second to wet both hands by gripping the wet mesh of the landing-net.

The very best net for retaining bream is the largest you can afford. It should be made from super-soft, knotless, nylon micro-mesh, which is the kindest material on the bream's delicate body and fins as they split all too easily.

The Steadefast 'protector' net is particularly good. It allows the catch to be released through the bottom by way of two clips that hold the last two rings together, not tumbled down the entire length of the net. These nets are available in 21-in round or 20 × 16-in rectangular frames with an angle-lock bankstick threaded tilt built into the 24-in top ring, and are 8–12 ft long.

Also recommended are Keepnets made by Keenets, which incorporate a soft nylon material with punched holes called 'safe flo' covering the bottom two rings, which provides a darker, less stressful environment than straightforward keepnet mesh. These micro/safe-flo mix nets are also available in both 20-in diameter round and

20 × 16-in rectangular formats and in lengths from 10 to 13 ft. Always purchase the largest you can afford. It will prove the best investment towards your future bream fishing.

Lastly, a simple but very effective tip to create even less stress to the fish inside: once the keep-net has been positioned and staked out (often necessary in strong winds), soak a soft, nylon carp-sack and lay it over the top of the last few rings protruding above the surface. The dark material will protect the bream inside from harsh sunlight and cut out unnatural shadows, allowing them to rest peacefully.

CHAPTER FIVE

BAITS

WHEN serving my bream-fishing apprenticeship way back in the mid-1950s, the accepted bait was either a bunch of maggots or a knob of bread paste on the hook, presented over a heavy carpet of groundbait. Generations of angling writers even implied that unless heavy groundbaiting was carried out, the bream simply would not respond; and everyone had their favourite additives, including potato peelings, for ensuring it was suitably stodgy. In those days, when the bream shoals in the UK's major river systems contained many more fish than they do today, the advice was probably sound. Indeed, when bream fishing in Ireland, Denmark, Sweden and Holland, where shoals are truly massive, heavy pre-baiting (see p. 74) is often imperative for success.

However, when shoal members can be counted in dozens rather than hundreds or thousands – as is the case throughout many hard-fished waters in England – the quickest way to stop them feeding, prevent them from starting to feed, or put them off moving into the swim, is to introduce more feed than the shoal requires. Try to anticipate the numbers of bream likely to be present wherever you fish, and if in doubt, introduce less rather than more whether using loose feed or groundbait. Remember, too, that a shoal of 200 good-sized bream that greedily mopped up a bucket of stodge during the summer, when their metabolic rate was at its highest, can be kept actively interested during a cold winter's day by little more than the occasional handful of loose feed such as maggots or casters.

To the inexperienced it hardly seems logical that a bream which wolfs down a thumbnail-sized lump of bread flake on a size 6 hook in July can be so undecided about sucking in a single caster on a tiny size 18 hook in January. However, water temperature, air temperature, or a mixture of both, dictates the bream's activity.

A general yardstick to apply is that as the water

temperature increases, bream are more liable to go for larger hook baits. Similarly, as it decreases they seem more attracted by smaller offerings presented on finer tackle. Although I have caught the odd bream on prawns meant for barbel, mini-boilies offered to tench, and even the insides of a whole swan mussel intended for catfish, in general terms, the bream is not as catholic in its tastes as the chub or carp. Notwithstanding the occasional fluke on a different offering, I suggest that the following armoury of baits will catch bream of all sizes from wherever you fish.

In sub-zero conditions bream bite extremely gently and will, on most occasions, only show interest in small baits like maggots and casters, a fact of which Bob Nudd is only too aware. Hence his total concentration on the quivertip for those gentle drop-back bites.

BREAD

In any of its forms bread is certainly one of the most effective bream baits in summer when nuisance fish like immature roach or rudd become attracted to small, natural baits such as maggots and casters. Moreover, wherever perch are thick on the ground and making it impossible to offer maggots, and particularly worms, to bream, bread will take you straight to the better-quality bream. Bread is also an excellent bait for river fishing at night during the summer, when anything of a meaty nature lying on the bottom very soon receives the attention of eels.

Bread flake

Bread flake taken from the inside of a new white loaf (ready-sliced or a tin) swells in the water and becomes fluffy around the edges – a bait which bream adore. The loaf must be fresh and doughy, or the flake will crumble and fall off the hook after a short time. I find that sliced loaves wrapped in a polybag last noticeably longer than tin loaves, but the choice is a personal one. When white is not available, I happily catch bream on brown bread, though the special yeast in white bread helps the flake to stay longer on the hook.

To ensure that flake stays on during the longest casts and remains on for several minutes afterwards, even in running water, fold a large piece around the hook and pinch tightly between thumb and forefinger only along the shank and around the eye. This allows the flake which has not been compressed to fluff out and hide both point and barb without impairing penetration on the most gentle of strikes. Once you have mastered this, you will never be the slightest bit worried about whether your flake is still on the hook after casting. Experiment using only fresh bread until you acquire that kind of confidence.

As a change from completely covering the hook, bread flake works wonderfully in a cocktail with other baits. Try for instance two maggots, two grains of corn or stewed wheat, or half a worm on the bend of the hook, with a piece of flake pinched along the shank. Never be shy to experiment, because when bream are in a particularly dour mood, something a little different is often enough to excite an immediate response.

Bread paste

The best paste should have a creamy, lump-free consistency, and is best made from old bread, of at least 3 to 4 days old. Cut off the crusts and immerse the bread for a few seconds under the cold tap. With clean hands, start kneading and continue until all the excess water and stickiness have gone, leaving a smooth, pliable paste. This stays on the hook well, and the hook can easily pull through it on the strike.

I prefer plain bread paste, but there is no reason why you cannot experiment by kneading in a small quantity of grated cheese or sausage-meat. A teaspoonful of custard powder, which turns the paste a subtle yellow, is a ruse that some bream fishermen swear by. A paste that has proved most successful over the years is made from equal amounts of bread paste and a paste made from ground-down trout pellets. Pelleted pond-fish food works just as efficiently, and if you cannot grind the pellets into dust, use the coffee-grinder, putting in the pellets a handful at a time. Transfer the ground-down pellets to a bowl and sprinkle liberally with hot water; leave for 30 minutes, until all the water has been absorbed. Then knead until creamy and mix thoroughly into the bread paste.

To compliment trout pellet paste on the hook, add at least 1–2 pt into the groundbait either as ground-down dust or as a sloppy mash (see 'Groundbaiting', p. 68–73).

Incidentally, paste keeps and travels better if it is made into a large ball and placed in a piece of dampened linen. If any appreciable amount is left unused, it can be wrapped tightly in a polybag and popped into the freezer.

Bread crust

While bread crust does not stay on the hook anywhere as long as either paste or flake, its extra buoyancy is extremely useful. A cube of crust ¼ or ½ in square presented on size 12 or 10 hooks respectively is the ideal bait when fishing over thick bottom-weed, as it will eventually come to rest gently on top of the weed rather than falling through it and becoming hidden, as other baits do. Similarly, an oblong of crust may be threaded along the shank and over the eye, providing buoyancy to cocktails. On the bend of the hook, try a small worm, corn, wheat, maggots or casters, or even a pinch of bread flake, to complete the cocktail.

A large piece of plain breadflake is a wonderful bream bait that, through size alone, generally attracts a larger-than-average bream. Bread cocktails work well, too. Try adding a couple of maggots, a brandling, or two corn kernels to the bend of the hook before squeezing the flake around the shank.

Bream really do respond to the buoyancy in crust, probably because it behaves so naturally as it wavers gently about near the bottom, just like other fragments of bread-based groundbait being continually whisked up by the fins of fish feeding aggressively.

NATURALS

Maggots

The humble, shop-bought maggot (which comes from the second most-common European bluebottle) is, of course, the most popular of all bream baits, and rightly so. Apart from being cheap and always readily available, bream love the taste and craftily suck out the inside juices by squeezing the maggot between their pharyngeal teeth. When the maggot comes back as a skin, decidedly 'stretched', this is what has happened, and you will have missed a positive bite. If ledgering, reduce the hook length until you see a hittable bite on the indicator; if floatfishing, move the bottom shot closer to the hook so that you see the bite sooner. It is as simple as that.

When bream are coming really thick and fast to bunches of maggots, don't worry too much about leaving skins on the hook. A combination of two or three skins, plus two

The question of whether the colour of a maggot makes any significant difference always gives rise to an interesting discussion among bream fishermen. Bronze or red are favoured by the author.

Don't bother changing over to fresh maggots each cast when bream show a liking for bunches. A combination of sucked skins and live maggots often has more appeal.

All worms, brandlings in particular, are irresistable to bream. Note the delicate, fully protrusible mouth that extends to siphon up natural food particles such as bloodworms from the bottom sediment.

or three fresh maggots, often brings a more positive bite than a bunch of fresh maggots. Bream sometimes show a noticeable preference for coloured maggots as opposed to plain white. Bronze are good, and I particularly favour red. Whenever I have been bream fishing in Ireland and Denmark, where the waters have a distinct 'peaty' hue, red maggots have proved to be most effective, either in a bunch or used 'cocktail' fashion in conjunction with casters, sweetcorn or red worms.

While *squats* (the maggot of a small house-fly) and *pinkies* (the maggot of the greenbottle) have over the years become synonymous with bream fishing on the Fenland drains and throughout the Midlands, I must admit only to using pinkies occasionally, during the coldest of winter weather, when stepping down to ultra-fine tackle and hooks from a 20 upwards. Casters have, in fact, rather superceded small maggots in recent years as loose feed for bream.

The squat is still popular with match anglers fishing clear-water canals because being lighter, it falls slowly through the water and complements 'on the drop' techniques (see p. 76).

Gozzers, those soft, succulent maggots of the most common European bluebottle, are not readily available in tackle shops because they do not live happily indoors where all commercial maggots are bred. Although gozzers are exactly the same size as ordinary shop-bought maggots, bream like them because they are so soft. And no doubt there are times when this could make all the difference between bites and no bites. However, I could never be bothered with the rigmarole of breeding them at the bottom of the garden, and I have survived almost 40 years of catching bream on maggots purchased from the tackle shop without ever sticking a hook into a gozzer.

Casters

Casters are an exceptionally fine bream bait, both on the hook and when added to the groundbait as an attractor. For fishing over dense bottom-weed, the darker (more buoyant) ones work best, whether presented singly on a size 18, two up on a size 14, or in a bunch covering a size 12 or 10 hook. Caster and maggot, caster and corn, and caster and worm cocktails all catch bream too.

For clear-water conditions, when bream are particularly finicky on the float, a single caster presented among small quantities of loose feed is a deadly bait. Ensure that the small hook (sizes 18 to 22) is gently buried into the caster through one end, and not piercing the side of the shell that can then be easily crushed by the bream's pharyngeal teeth – by which time, of course, you should have struck. In fact, because casters are so easily crushed (often without the angler being aware of it), to use only casters on the hook when ledgering can prove rather frustrating. You might even find yourself sitting there, having been castorized by the bream with nothing but remnants of the shells on the hook. The answer is to make the bream hold on longer by using cocktails when ledgering, so do not be afraid to experiment.

Worms

A big lobworm is not only one of the most selective baits for specimen bream, worms in general are magic for attracting only bream when the swim is choc-a-block full with small shoal fish like roach, which always seem to reach baits such as maggots or casters first.

You should never set off for a day's bream fishing without a good supply of worms, and fair-sized brandlings have the edge in pulling power over ordinary earthworms. It is that smelly, yellow liquid emanating from the brandling that is found in muck heaps, and the lively way in which they wriggle on the hook, which really turns bream on. Time and time again, in water that is either gin-clear or heavily coloured (through flooding), after experiencing mediocre results with a lump of bread flake or maggots I have switched over to a gyrating bunch of brandlings, which have met an immediate response.

For the super-wary bream of clear-watered lakes and gravel pits during the early summer, when an abundance of natural food is at their disposal, a bunch of brandlings fished on the drop beneath a self-cocking float is often the only route to success. It goes without saying of course, that worm and maggot, worm and caster or worm and corn are cocktails that bream rarely refuse. Always remember to hook the worm on first, once only, through the middle – three brandlings on a size 12 or 10, followed by a single grain of corn or two maggots. The worms cannot then possibly wriggle off over the barb.

PARTICLES

Stewed wheat

Like the seed of all grasses that are deposited quite unthought-of distances by the wind or in the crops of birds, wheat is no stranger to bream feeding along the margins of lakes, meres and rivers fringed by farmland. Next to worms, it is perhaps the most common of all the natural baits they regularly see during the summer months. Yet I will wager that the majority of bream fishermen have never caught one on stewed wheat.

As you can purchase a 100-lb sack of wheat, which suffices for hook bait, loose feed and part of the groundbait, for the price of 3 pt of maggots, it makes sense to pay the local corn chandler a visit when thinking about summer bream fishing. To prepare a small quantity of wheat for hook baits, that old tip of putting a handful into a thermos flask, topping up with boiling water and leaving overnight, is fine – as long as you allow space at the top for massive expansion or the flask will blow up. Wheat swells to three times its size when stewed, to about the size of large sweetcorn, and has a most distinctive, 'nutty' aroma much to the liking of bream.

To prepare large quantities, put the wheat into a large bucket with a rip-off lid, and cover in volume with twice as much boiling water. Press the lid on firmly and leave for 24 hours, whereupon any excess water can be strained off. The swollen grains, now split at one end revealing the soft white inside (the flour), can either be used immediately or packed into polybags and put in the freezer for future sessions. I endeavour to fish with this bait freshly prepared because its distinctive aroma makes it so effective.

Wheat is very easy to colour. Simply add a large spoonful of powder carp-bait dye when pouring on the

boiling water and stir gently before fixing on the lid. My preference is for yellow or red, but there is nothing to stop you experimenting with this fabulous bait for tench, carp, chub or barbel. Roach and rudd love it too.

Whether you are float or ledger fishing, wheat is best presented as one grain on a size 14, two on a size 12, or three up on a size 10 or an 8. Ensure the point and barb emerge through the soft centre for good penetration on the strike.

One of the most effective and certainly the cheapest of summer bream baits is stewed wheat. On the rod of Charlie Clay it led to the downfall of this fine 9 lb, Norfolk gravel-pit specimen.

Sweetcorn

Like most summer species that acquire a taste for sweet-corn, bream respond really well to this most convenient bait. In certain fisheries, stillwaters in particular, sweetcorn can prove as instant with bream as with tench and carp. In rivers, however, a certain amount of pre-baiting may be necessary in order to wean the bream on to it.

As several handfuls will be required for adding to the groundbait, in addition to hook baits, plus extra for catapulting out as loose feed, purchase sweetcorn in bulk freezer packs, which is considerably cheaper than one tin at a time. That which is not used can be put back into the freezer in a polybag.

Use corn kernels singly on a size 14, two up on a size 12, and so on. To offer a really large mouthful, thread two or three kernels up and over the eye of a size 8 or 6 hook before slipping three on the bend. Then gently slide the others down so they come to rest against the first ones, thus completely covering the shank.

Sweetcorn can be dyed (using a carp-bait powder dye in conjunction with a little hot water) to extend its effective life once bream start to wise up. You will know when this happens because the numbers of bites expected in a session, even for prolific waters, will drastically slow up. I prefer to switch over to another bait when this situation develops, or to step down to smaller hooks and lighter hook lengths, but experimenting with varying colours, and even adding a different smell to the corn, can be fun. The range of bait flavourings available nowadays is unbelievably extensive. Simply strain off all fluid with the corn and put into a clean polybag. Then add a teaspoonful of flavour, tie up the bag and shake vigorously. Leave for a couple of hours for the flavour to be absorbed and use straight from the bag.

GROUNDBAITING

The very term groundbaiting can, I admit, seem rather misleading to the uninitiated. Handfuls of sweetcorn or stewed wheat thrown regularly into the swim as loose feed is a form of groundbait. However, as far as this book is concerned, let us think of groundbait as bulk preparation of a cereal base to which various ingredients are added, including fragments of the intended hook bait.

As both mashed bread and dry breadcrumbs originate from wheat flour, they are cereal bases, as is maize meal, and that old bream-fisher's favourite 'layers mash', to which bran is added for stiffening. I still think bread makes by far the best groundbait for bream, and recommend that you stick with it as a base, adding other ingredients particular to the situation at hand.

It is well to remember that there are no secret groundbait ingredients that will make bream crawl up the rod. The key is in what you use, and the consistency to which it is mixed – hard, firm, or as a cloud, for example.

Let us consider a swim in Ireland's mighty River Shannon, for instance, where just 30 ft out from the bank the flow is often quite strong with the bottom shelving away to a staggering depth of over 20 ft. It would be a complete waste of time lobbing out half-a-dozen balls of sloppy, cloud-type groundbait and expect to attract a shoal of adult bream (which in the Shannon could be anything up to several hundred fish in the 3–6 lb class). Bream such as these need feeding to hold them in the swim. In fact, pre-baiting for a couple of evenings, before commencing to fish on the second morning, is the best plan of action (see 'Pre-baiting', p. 73–5). Such is the size and depth of the river.

Bread crumbs

Plain breadcrumbs mixed with just enough water to hold them together makes the perfect base. To stiffen the mixture for throwing, I recommend that you add 2 pt of pearl barley per bucket of bait, plus several handfuls of the intended hook bait, such as worm fragments, maggots, sweetcorn, casters or stewed wheat, once the crumbs have been dampened. As an alternative to pearl barley, which really locks the crumb together and takes the balls of groundbait down quickly, try flaked maize. Looking rather like industrial cornflakes, flaked maize is a great binder, especially when using sweetcorn on the hook

While bream fishing in the beautiful complex of interconnecting lakes near Silkeborg in Denmark, international match fisherman, Dave Thomas, knows full well that to keep the massive shoals of bream interested, regular groundbaiting throughout the day is imperative.

because it comes from maize's sister plant and has that similar, golden-yellow colour and distinctive aroma. The bream will then be very much quicker on to your hook bait.

Mashed bread

For stillwaters or slow-moving rivers, where it is desirable for the groundbait to break up quickly during those last few feet before it hits bottom, I like to use mashed bread as a base. Old bread is best, and I make a point of keeping all bread scraps in an old keep-net hanging in the garage for this purpose. Soak the scraps for a couple of hours in a tub of cold water, then strain off the excess water and squeeze it between your hands into a pulp. It can then be stiffened with maize meal, bran, or even dry breadcrumbs. In fact any brand of packeted, shop-bought groundbait can be used – plus, of course, some hook-bait fragments.

If the mixture needs to be moulded into firm balls for throwing (tangerine-sized balls throw best) or catapulting

To ensure that the sandwich of loose feed and breadcrumbs really explodes from an open-ended plastic swimfeeder as it hits bottom, Bob Nudd just dampens the coarse crumbs.

distances beyond that of an underarm lob, further binding is required. Add 2 pt of flaked maize to a bucket of groundbait. The beauty of mashed bread groundbait is that it sinks well and disintegrates into a million varying-sized particles, attracting but not drastically overfeeding the fish.

Extra additives

For use in still and slow-moving waters, boiled rice is an excellent additive that keeps bream hoovering away at the individual grains hour after hour. Stewed hempseed is another mass particle well worth trying, as is crushed hempseed, an ingredient present in many of today's proprietory pre-packeted groundbaits. I rate stewed wheat as one of the finest bulk additives, particularly during the summer months when large bream shoals are capable of consuming vast quantities of food. Even when using bread flake, paste or crust on the hook, I feel more confident with a few fragments of alternative hook baits mixed into the groundbait. I can then change over at any time, knowing the bream will have tried them already. Casters and sweetcorn go well together, as do maggots and brandlings, or stewed wheat and lobworm halves – the choice is yours. Or you could mix them all in together, if you like. That is the fun of experimenting with groundbaits, as long as you do not draw any hard-and-fast conclusions from the results. If you are planning to use trout pellet paste on the hook, 1–2 pt of ground-down trout pellets, pond fish food or salmon fry crumbs should go into the base mix.

Lighter groundbaits

Although bucketfuls of groundbait may sometimes be needed on big rivers and stillwaters in order to hold large shoals of adult bream, there are numerous situations when a smaller quantity will be most effective. In cold-water conditions, such as in the late autumn and throughout the winter months; in swims containing only limited numbers of bream; in clear-water conditions when the fish are spooky, and so on; at such times, vast amounts of stodge in the water will lessen your chances of success, not improve them. If you are in any doubt about how much and how often, adopt a leaf from the roach fisherman's book. 'Little and often' works for bream too.

Lighter mixes that break up quickly and attract rather than feed are made from fine breadcrumbs, to which water is added slowly, a little at a time. Use a shallow mixing-bowl or groundbait tray for this job, and keep fluffing the crumbs about with your spare hand while adding the water from a maggot tin with the other. It is interesting to note that top-class match fishermen almost to the man prefer brown crumb for their lighter bream feed, and are particularly fussy about hard lumps. These are riddled off with a groundbait sieve and discarded before the final mixing stage, when a handful of clean hook bait is added. If it is prepared perfectly, a handful of this lighter mix, squeezed together hard, will go straight down and only break up on the bottom. Yet if it is squeezed gently, it will separate beautifully into an attractive cloud the moment it hits surface. In very shallow swims this is more advantageous, as it is when presenting the hook bait on the drop. It is a really versatile groundbait suitable for all depths and situations where huge shoals are not expected.

I have my own preference for making a similar, lighter cloud-type groundbait, again with fine breadcrumbs. I am not fussy whether they are white or brown, and it allows me to use up any old casters that are beyond redemption as hook baits. I do not care whether they are floaters, or how much they stink (indeed I even think that stinking casters add more attraction), I grind them to a pulp a handful at a time over the groundbait tray, using their juices to dampen the breadcrumbs while adding millions of brown caster-shell particles for visual effect. It makes a really super cloud groundbait to which a little water may have to be added. Try it and see.

Another ruse for accentuating the cloud of groundbait is to add some evaporated milk, which really does produce an amazing effect. And of course, there is nothing to stop you colouring the entire mix with a large spoonful of powder carp-bait dye.

Feeder groundbait

By far the best groundbait for use with wire, cage-type feeders, is a very lightly dampened mix of coarse bread-crumbs, to which a few fragments of the hook bait should be added. This mixture explodes and scatters only upon reaching the bottom, not prematurely.

An even better method, but one which can only be used with plastic open-ended feeders, is to fill the middle of the feeder with loose-feed hook baits and plug each end with dampened, coarse breadcrumbs. It takes a few seconds longer than filling cage-type feeders, but deposits more hook-bait samples on the bottom.

PRE-BAITING

As I mentioned at the start of this chapter, pre-baiting is often a prerequisite for catching bream that inhabit large, deep and wide rivers and huge stillwaters. Even during the

Don't throw away old floating or even sinking casters. Take a tip from John and squeeze them into a pulp, using the juices plus a little water to dampen breadcrumb groundbait into balls ready for throwing.

summer months the shoals are seldom scattered evenly like currants in a well-baked cake, and unless you have attracted a shoal or two in advance, you could be fishing several hundred yards away from the nearest bream. This is by far the most common fault among anglers who pilgrimage across the sea to bream-fish Ireland's huge loughs, or the lakes of Sweden and Denmark. They flit from one spot to another instead of pre-baiting a couple of areas and waiting for the bream to move in.

If I were contemplating fishing for bream in a large expanse of water not regularly fished, where the bream have not become used to the introduction of free food along the margins of certain areas, I would plan a pre-baiting campaign. If the shoals are numerically strong, with individual fish on the large side, I would introduce a bucket of groundbait laced with hook-bait fragments into the chosen swim every other day for a week. This I would do at dusk so as not to attract the attentions of diving water-birds and other anglers. In the meantime, I would keep a very close eye, with binoculars, on the swim each morning for signs that the bream had located the food – the occasional porpoising fish or bubble trails littering the surface – before thinking about fishing.

There is, of course, no reason why you cannot keep several pre-baiting stints going at the same time in different parts of the lake or river to see what transpires. You could hedge your bets further by pre-baiting several

different locations at the same time. It need not necessarily cost a fortune. I have already mentioned the cheapness of wheat against other baits, and perhaps a polite enquiry at the local bakers, cake shop, supermarket or cafeteria might result in regular batches of unsaleable items that can be crushed and used as a cereal base.

In complete contrast, to attract the attention of, say, a small group of large bream that are clearly visible in a deep hole or junction-swim on a small, clear-flowing, weedy river, all you need do is introduce a couple of handfuls of stewed wheat, sweetcorn or mashed bread each evening as dusk falls.

Do not attempt to pre-bait with maggots. They are too attractive to small shoal species (and eels) and could, if not eaten quickly, wriggle out of sight into the bottom sediment.

Proof of the importance of pre-baiting overnight when seeking the bream of large stillwaters. Terry Smith and John team up to take this huge bream haul from Garadice Lake while filming for the Irish Tourist Board.

CHAPTER SIX

TECHNIQUES AND RIGS

WAGGLER-STYLE FLOATFISHING

The most sensitive method of catching bream in stillwaters is to present the bait close to or actually static on the bottom with light float tackle. For calm conditions when bream are situated or can be drawn close in, say within two rod lengths, the ideal float is a slim–tipped antenna, such as the 'stillwater green'.

Stillwater green rig

After plummeting the depth carefully, set the float slightly deeper than the swim by locking the bulk shot on either side of the bottom ring, leaving just two small shots to go down the line, with the last few inches of line and bait lying on the bottom (fig. 7A). If you use a swivel float attachment, into which the bottom of the float easily pushes, you can make a quick change of float should wind conditions change or you choose to fish further out.

The remaining two small shots, Nos. 6 or 8, are positioned to function in two distinct ways: to determine bites from bream that swim directly away from the rod, causing the fine float-tip to sink and slowly disappear; and to indicate those bites when small baits such as casters and maggots are sucked in while they are sinking (on the drop) (fig. 7B). In the latter situation, the biting fish holds up that all-important bottom shot, so whenever the float-tip fails to settle in the lowest position in the water at the moment it should, a confident strike can be made.

If the bait is not taken on the drop, but lies untouched on the bottom for several minutes, one ruse that sometimes instigates an immediate response from lethargic bream is

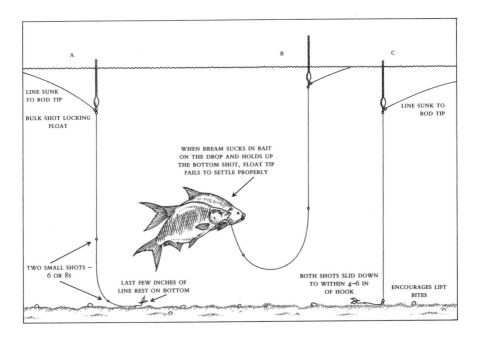

A

LINE SUNK
TO ROD TIP

BULK SHOT LOCKING
FLOAT

WHEN BREAM SUCKS IN BAIT
ON THE DROP AND HOLDS UP
THE BOTTOM SHOT, FLOAT TIP
FAILS TO SETTLE PROPERLY

B

C

LINE SUNK TO
ROD TIP

TWO SMALL SHOTS –
6 OR 8s

LAST FEW INCHES OF
LINE REST ON BOTTOM

BOTH SHOTS SLID DOWN
TO WITHIN 4–6 IN
OF HOOK

ENCOURAGES LIFT
BITES

to wind the float quickly towards you, a foot or two at a time. This momentarily whisks the bait attractively upwards, allowing it to freefall again. Bream really go for this in clear-water conditions.

Light baits, such as a single caster on a size 20 hook, fall much more slowly and thus more naturally on a finer hook length. Therefore, if bites are not forthcoming with a bigger bait and larger hook tied direct to a 2 or 3 lb reel line, step down to a more natural presentation. Even bream up to 3 lb can be comfortably handled on a 1-lb bottom, so experiment whenever bites are not occurring but you are certain bream are in the swim.

When bream are packed tightly together, feeding in earnest from the carpet of groundbait or loose feed on the bottom, lack of space may prevent them from moving off with the bait and providing you with a sailaway bite on the float-tip. Instead, with their bodies angled downwards and their protrusible mouths fully extended, they hoover up food and right themselves to chew on the spot.

By far the best shotting pattern to indicate this kind of bite is to slide both shots down to within 4–6 in from the hook (fig. 7C). The bait is now anchored and presented lift-style – when the bream sucks it up and rights itself, thus dislodging the shots, the float-tip rises in a glorious lift. To

FIGURE 7 *Stillwater green rig*

John's waggler rod in action while making a Go Fishing TV programme in the Danish Lakelands. Most of the shotting load was bulked 10 in from the hook to take the bait straight down through a myriad of small roach and rudd to the bream on the bottom.

encourage more deliberate float-tip indications, do not be afraid to juggle about with that all-important distance between hook and bottom shots. I have, on occasions, moved them to within only 1 in of the hook and struck successfully at the tiniest suggestion of the float-tip rising.

Tipped (insert) peacock waggler rig

For presenting the bait beyond distances of two rod lengths into stillwater, you need floats capable of carrying additional casting shot, and there is nothing to beat the tipped (insert) peacock waggler. Tipped wagglers, just like stillwater greens, are locked by the bulk shot at slightly more than swim depth. And with the line sunk to alleviate surface drift, the bait is presented in the same fashion as for a 'stillwater green'. Make a practice of casting several yards beyond the swim, then pushing the rod tip quickly below the surface and cranking the reel handle a few turns to ensure that all the line is sunk, before lifting the tip clear and holding it steady 6 in above the surface.

I cannot stress enough the importance of this simple manoeuvre. It makes the difference between the bait behaving as naturally as the loose feed around it and behaving completely unnaturally, as happens when the wind pulls a floating line and thus the bait along the bottom. Keep a small bottle of neat washing-up liquid handy in the tackle bag, and smear some around the spool occasionally. This helps new monofilament, especially, to cut through the surface film and sink instantly.

Another factor to consider when all the line is sunk beneath the surface film is that the effectiveness of an upwards strike is greatly reduced. Because of the effect of surface tension, it is much easier to pull the line through the water than to lift it off the surface. So when waggler fishing (and the further out, the more critical this becomes) endeavour always to strike sideways and not directly upwards. You will notice how smoothly the float folds, and feel the cushioning effect of a sideways strike low to the water.

Start with the shotting pattern in fig. 8A, the bulk shots locking the float and two small shots down the line – say, a No. 1 and then a No. 6 – with the last few inches of line lying along the bottom. If a bream sucks in the bait on the drop, the lower shot's descent through the water is held up and the float-tip fails to settle when it should: strike immediately. If a bream sucks up the bait and moves slowly away, however, the tip of the float simply disappears from view.

One of the problems encountered while after the better-quality bream in a swim full of mixed sizes, where small bream plus roach or rudd occupy the upper water layers, stems from an over-sensitive shotting pattern, which allows smaller fish to intercept the bait on the way down. Rearrange the shotting load to take the bait straight down to the bottom on to the noses of the larger bream. Move

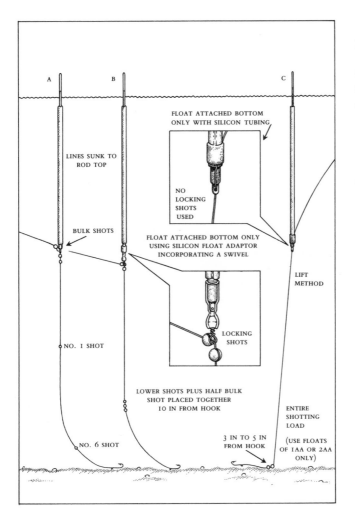

FIGURE 8 *Tipped (insert) peacock wagglers – for close to medium range in stillwaters*

A   B   C

LINES SUNK TO ROD TOP

FLOAT ATTACHED BOTTOM ONLY WITH SILICON TUBING

NO LOCKING SHOTS USED

BULK SHOTS

FLOAT ATTACHED BOTTOM ONLY USING SILICON FLOAT ADAPTOR INCORPORATING A SWIVEL

LIFT METHOD

LOCKING SHOTS

NO. I SHOT

LOWER SHOTS PLUS HALF BULK SHOT PLACED TOGETHER 10 IN FROM HOOK

ENTIRE SHOTTING LOAD

NO. 6 SHOT

3 IN TO 5 IN FROM HOOK

(USE FLOATS OF IAA OR 2AA ONLY)

half the bulk shots from around the float and group them with the lower shots just 10 in from the hook (fig. 8B). This may seem rather crude, but with a swim full of varying-sized fish it is one of only two ways to get through the nuisance species. The other way is to change the bait size. If bites from small fish persist, try going up in hook size to a bunch of maggots or a piece of bread flake on a size 10, or a cocktail of a whole lobworm or bunch of brandlings with sweetcorn crammed on to a size 8. Dispense with a light bottom by tying the hook direct to the reel line. Bream are far less suspicious of terminal tackle when sucking in larger mouthfuls (see 'Baits' for various options).

Lift method

Wagglers carrying between one and two AA shots are perfect to use for the lift method (fig. 8C). The lift is really only effective at short range – up to about two rod lengths out. This is because the line must angle upwards from float to rod tip, and the strike must also be made upwards, in contrast to general waggler techniques, when the line is sunk and the strike consists of a sideways pull.

Being an exceptionally deep-bodied fish, the adult bream gives wonderfully accentuated lift or flat-float bites when returning to the horizontal, having sucked in the bait from the bottom. The float instantly keels over, almost flying upwards to lie flat as though the shots have completely gone or someone has mysteriously cut the line. At this point the bream is supporting the shots, so strike at once before it ejects the bait. Better still, with those lovely slow lifts as the quill rises perpendicularly before tilting over, is to anticipate a bite by holding the rod and slamming the hook home while the float is rising.

To counteract any slight draw on the surface, set the float about 1 ft over-depth, so it lies flat once the shots have settled on the bottom. Then, with the rod tip angled upwards to keep any line between it and the float off the surface, slowly wind in line until the float cocks. In flat calm conditions, wind down until only the merest blimp of the insert tip is showing; when the surface is broken, ensure that the entire insert is visible.

The lift at night

Because bites are indicated so deliberately with the lift method, it is without doubt the best rig for night fishing. Simply fix a mini luminous starlight element to the insert tip with the sleeve of silicon tubing supplied. Starlights, which last for around 8 hours and work by chemical activation when you bend and then shake one, are available in varying diameters and lengths to suit the float-tip being used. For ease of visibility throughout a long, all-night session, the tipped waggler may be swapped for a straight waggler, which has an appreciably thicker top and can take the largest starlight.

Do not worry too much about super-sensitivity at night. Bream bite far more boldly than they do during daylight, particularly in crystal-clear water. Indeed, I know several clear-water lakes and pits holding limited numbers of very large specimen bream, where I have never managed to persuade them to accept a baited hook until darkness falls. They then become ridiculously easy to catch.

Plain peacock-quill stems (these are occasionally available from tackle shops and wild-life parks) are better suited to lift fishing than commercially-produced straight wagglers. I keep a tubeful of 12-in long plain stems of various diameters from super-thin to thick, all with the ends painted a fluorescent matt red. I select one to suit the shots required for reaching the bream easily, attach it to the line with a thick band of silicon tubing, and with a pair of scissors snip pieces off the bottom end until the red tip sits perfectly above the surface when cocked by the shots.

A luminous starlight is fitted in a jiffy with the silicon tubing supplied. You have another night-fishing waggler option when using Drennan crystal waggler floats, all of which have removable insert tips. You simply change the coloured insert tip for a luminous night-light tip (which has the same luminosity as, and is almost identical to, the starlight). These plug quickly into Drennan's range of giant insert crystals, the slim insert crystal and the bodied crystals, which provide greater stability in really gusty conditions.

Overleaf In cold, swirling water bream demand a static bait. Andy Jubb of Norwich holds the rod steady while keeping a watchful eye on the float. He is stret pegging a deep marginal run close beside a bed of decaying bullrush stems for the large bream inhabiting this Norfolk mill-pool.

The waggler in moving water

Use of the waggler in running water provides a choice between anchoring the bait to the bottom or presenting it trundling slowly over the river-bed at current pace. And for both methods the straight peacock waggler is best, because unlike the insert waggler, whose tip is drawn under too easily, its inherent buoyancy allows small baits to be trundled smoothly over an uneven bottom without the tip dragging under and registering false bites.

For dragging small baits like casters or maggots along the bottom in very slow currents, group most of the bulk

shot around the float, which should be set at least 1 ft over-
depth. Then dot several small shots at equal distances (say,
every 18–20 in) down the line, finishing with a dust shot
(fig. 9A). For the best presentation in windy weather, sink
the line as though fishing in stillwater and strike sideways.
In calm conditions ensure that the line floats, allowing
reasonable slack and a distinct bow from float to rod tip so
that the bait is not drawn inwards and away from the feed
line.

FIGURE 9 *The*
waggler in running
water 1

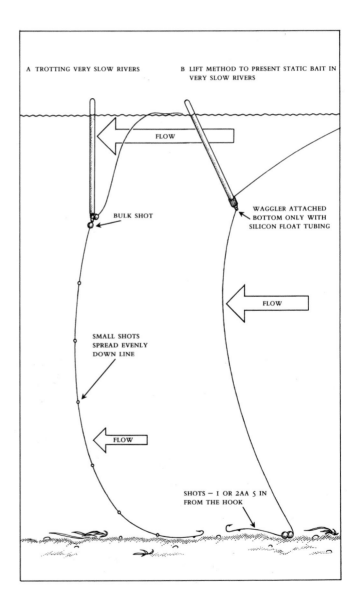

A TROTTING VERY SLOW RIVERS

B LIFT METHOD TO PRESENT STATIC BAIT IN
VERY SLOW RIVERS

FLOW

WAGGLER ATTACHED
BOTTOM ONLY WITH
SILICON FLOAT TUBING

BULK SHOT

FLOW

SMALL SHOTS
SPREAD EVENLY
DOWN LINE

FLOW

SHOTS – 1 OR 2AA 5 IN
FROM THE HOOK

For those occasions when bream refuse to accept a moving bait and show interest only in one lying static, put your faith in the lift method (fig. 9B). Set the float at least 2 ft over-depth to account for the flow, with the shots 5 in from the hook. Remember to keep the line angled upwards off the surface from float to rod tip or the flow will push the float-tip under. Bites will register as dramatic vertical lifts of the waggler, or a slow, ponderous disappearance should the bream turn downstream and away with the

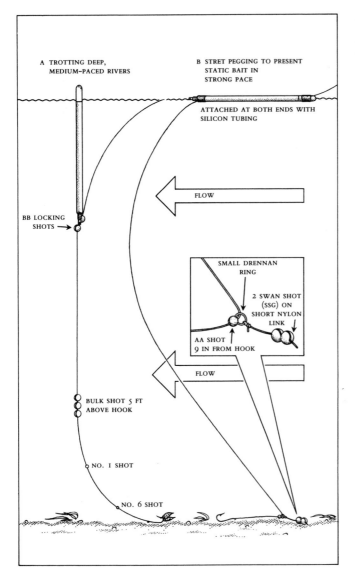

FIGURE 10 *The waggler in running water 2*

A TROTTING DEEP, MEDIUM-PACED RIVERS

B STRET PEGGING TO PRESENT STATIC BAIT IN STRONG PACE

ATTACHED AT BOTH ENDS WITH SILICON TUBING

FLOW

BB LOCKING SHOTS →

SMALL DRENNAN RING

2 SWAN SHOT (SSG) ON SHORT NYLON LINK

AA SHOT 9 IN FROM HOOK

FLOW

BULK SHOT 5 FT ABOVE HOOK

NO. 1 SHOT

NO. 6 SHOT

Ray Bows displays not a bream, but a superb bream/rudd hybrid, caught from a weir-pool eddy in southern Ireland on the waggler and a bunch of maggots tripping bottom.

bait. I particularly favour the lift when using large baits such as bread flake, paste or crust because bites are so positive.

To offer a moving bait in deep rivers of medium pace or deep eddies in weir-pools, choose a waggler carrying a fair shotting capacity – certainly of two swan shots plus – and after using a pair of BBs for locking it slightly over-depth, fix the bulk shot 5 ft above the hook. Finish with two small shots, such as a No. 1 and No. 6, between the bulk shot and the hook (fig. 10A).

To ensure that the bait lies perfectly static in strong currents and in low temperatures, the stret-pegging rig (fig. 10B) is recommended. However, you can only really use it in deep runs or holes situated close into the bank, no more than a rod length out. Attach the straight peacock waggler both top and bottom with silicon tubing and set it several feet over-depth. Pinch the bulk shot tightly on to 1–2 in of thick line, to which you tie a small Drennan ring (this is really a sliding mini-ledger). This is stopped with an AA shot 6–9 in from the hook.

Always make the cast downstream and slightly across, and put the rod in two rests with the tip angled upwards so that most of the line from float to tip is off the surface. The float will then come to rest lying flat, swaying gently from side to side. This set-up may seem insensitive. However, because the float lies flat rather than being cocked, bream do not feel any inhibitive buoyancy and therefore bite positively; sometimes the float slides slowly beneath the surface, following a little shaking, which indicates that the bream is mouthing the bait.

Stret-pegging works wonderfully well in conjunction with a carpet of maggots or casters deposited on the bottom by a bait-dropper, and lends itself well to attacking difficult river swims such as small, deep gullies, junction swims and the like – in fact, any marginal hot-spot where the shoal is confined to a small, known area.

Laying-on with the waggler

This technique is ideal for deep, slow-moving water and does exactly what its name implies. It permits the bait to be presented 'laying-on' over bottom weeds such as the sub-surface cabbage of the yellow water-lily, instead of falling through them and thus being hidden from feeding bream.

Because of heavy boat traffic on sluggish rivers like the Thames and Great Ouse, entire stretches exist where few of the common yellow water-lily flowers and pads ever grace the surface. Yet the entire bottom along the marginal shelf is carpeted in their soft lettuce-like leaves – better known as cabbages. Indeed, many anglers consider cabbage-patches a separate plant, but they are simply the sub-surface leaves of lilies that never reach the surface.

You need a very long waggler to fish this method effectively. It should carry two or three swan shot and be attached bottom end only with silicon tubing. Set it at least 2 ft deeper than the swim. About 18 in above the hook, join a 2-ft shot link to the reel line with a four-turn water knot; on to the end of this (just like a fixed paternoster ledger) go the swan shots (fig. 11). They are not responsible for cocking the float, so you can use as many as you like to aid casting and provide the weight necessary to carry them down through the cabbage leaves to the river-bed. Tighten up quickly after casting so that the waggler cocks with a good inch of the tip above the surface. This ensures that the very last thing to settle is the bait, which

FIGURE 11 *Laying on with the waggler – in slow-moving water*

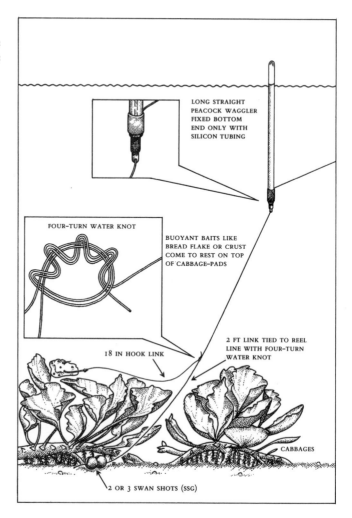

FIGURE 11 *Laying on with the waggler – in slow-moving water*

LONG STRAIGHT PEACOCK WAGGLER FIXED BOTTOM END ONLY WITH SILICON TUBING

FOUR-TURN WATER KNOT

BUOYANT BAITS LIKE BREAD FLAKE OR CRUST COME TO REST ON TOP OF CABBAGE-PADS

18 IN HOOK LINK

2 FT LINK TIED TO REEL LINE WITH FOUR-TURN WATER KNOT

CABBAGES

2 OR 3 SWAN SHOTS (SSG)

will rest in full view on top of the cabbages, where the bream can see it. A large piece of fresh, white bread flake, pinched tightly in just one small area along the hook shank, comes to rest extremely gently. Also effective is a balanced offering of bread crust on the hook shank and flake on the bend. Even better still is a ½-in cube of plain bread crust tipped with a single maggot to make it gyrate enticingly.

In most cases a bite is registered by the long waggler slowly and confidently disappearing from view. A tip worth mentioning here with regard to the ensuing fight is to pinch the swan shots very lightly on to the end of the link so that, should the bream become snagged, they will pull off and allow you to land it.

POLE-FISHING

Because the line can be held immediately upstream, or even upwind, of the float without it being dragged under or off course (thus affecting bait presentation in distances of up to 30–40 ft out), the degree of sensitivity provided by pole-fishing has no equal. Only in extremely gusty conditions, or when you fancy a change, is it pertinent to sink the line and change tack to waggler fishing or ledgering.

The renowned short-line/long-pole method, using only 5–6 ft of line between float and pole-tip, is arguably the most deadly of all match-fishing techniques. Some anglers find the constant need to ship (take apart) the pole down to a length commensurate with swim depth rather a rigmarole. However, the results in terms of bait presentation can prove so rewarding that it is not an easy method to ignore. Equally, fishing in deep water or a fair way out (necessitating a rig length similar to that of the pole itself so that the hook comes neatly to hand), is also enjoyable, whether the pole is an expensive 40 ft carbon or a 6 m telescopic hollow-glass cheapy.

Still and slow-moving water

If a sensitive approach is required using small baits and hooks, as both clear-water and winter conditions in particular dictate, use an elasticated tip (see 'Poles', p. 37), which acts as a buffer against small hooks pulling out or a fine hook length snapping whenever the bream dives. The elasticated tip permits the use of extra-fine hook lengths down to 12 oz for those rare occasions when, unless you step down, the bream do not bite.

Oval-bodied, bristle-tipped pole floats show the tiniest of bites in still or slow-moving water, and unless the shoal is situated high in the water and bites on the drop are expected, concentrate the shotting capacity low down, with an olivette and a small shot spaced in 12-in intervals above the hook (fig. 12A).

Accurate plumbing of the swim is essential for this method, where the bait should be presented lying on the

FIGURE 12 *Pole*
fishing

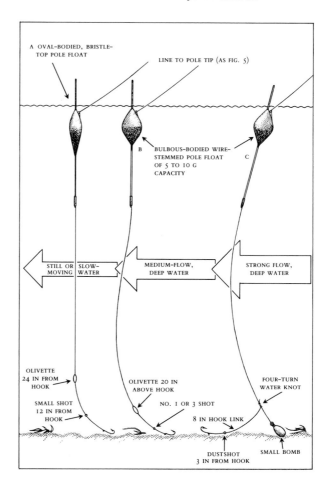

bottom by 1–2 in. To stimulate interest from bream that are slow on to the bait, raise the pole-tip 1 ft or so every so often to whisk the bait up from the bottom, encouraging it to freefall down again. And be ready for an immediate response as the float settles.

Keep either loose feed or small balls of cereal groundbait laced with maggots or casters going in close to the float with every put-in if you suspect the presence of a fair-sized shoal. During the summer months, small balls of cereal going into the swim on a regular basis are not liable to overfeed the fish. In the winter months, on the other hand, during sub-zero temperatures, especially when the water is on the clear side, half a dozen maggots accompanying each put-in, following perhaps an initial helping of two or three small balls of cereal food, will prove quite sufficient.

Using a 10-m
'to-hand rig' in a deep
stillwater, past master
with the pole and
international
matchwinner, Bob
Nudd, really enjoys
his bream fishing,
whatever the size of
the fish.

Accurate, regular
feeding around the
float with small,
maggot- or caster-laced
balls of cereal feed will
help to keep the bream
coming steadily when
you are pole fishing.
Only in really gusty
conditions will a
switch to the waggler
or quivertip rod
produce more fish.

Hit-and-hold tactics

Certain types of summer venues on stillwaters dictate that you must present the bait in among or alongside thick beds of tough lilies. For the inevitable hit-and-hold tussles which follow, a 5–6 m telescopic glass or glass/carbon-mix pole can be wound up nicely into a cushioning bend, dispensing with the need for shock-absorbing elastic. Such a tool may be held single-handed and supported along the forearm like a rod, and its soft action is your buffer and insurance against breakages.

A line of 3 or 4 lb test is tied directly to the tiny tip-ring. To minimize the danger of losing tackle you can dispense completely with specialized pole floats, and use a 3–5 in super-slim unpainted peacock quill attached bottom end only with silicon tubing instead. The float easily pulls out if the bream gets it head down and winds the float through a dense canopy of stems, flowers and pads. The quill is fished in the simple left method (see p. 81, fig. 8C), with one or two shots pinched on the line just 3–5 in from the hook, which is tied direct. When you have only adult, possibly specimen bream in mind, this is a fabulous way of offering them large baits like a whole lobworm, a lump of bread flake or four or five grains of corn, which are quickly taken down to the bottom through strands of soft weed and past the eyes of small, nuisance shoal fish.

Occasionally you may need to walk along the bank with a big bream hooked on such a set-up, but as a rule most fish are comfortably handled and subdued following an exciting fight. Part of the secret is that with the lift method you strike quickly enough (just as the float starts to rise) to hook the bream standing still, with its head off the bottom, and you can lever it away from potential snags before it realizes what is happening.

Deep, flowing water

My favourite two venues for taking bream beneath the pole-tip in deep, flowing water are both in Ireland: the lower reaches of the mighty River Shannon in southern

Ireland, where depths of 20 ft and more are the norm rather than the exception; and the prolific River Bann near Belfast in Northern Ireland, which flows through loughs Neagh and Beg. One's initial reaction is that such formidable waters are best attacked with the feeder rod; and overall, considering all water and weather conditions, perhaps the feeder does reign supreme. However, if you own a reasonably lightweight, rigid, carbon pole in the 9–12 m class, even swift-flowing swims can be fished comfortably.

Monstrous, bulbous-bodied pole floats with wire stems and carrying anything from 5 to 10 grams may seem over the top, but they are perfect for combatting deep water and strong, steady currents. Anything smaller would not allow the bait to be presented slowly enough. The object is to get the bait straight down to the bottom, either through unoccupied layers of water or through shoals of unwanted species such as small roach and rudd, then ease it back gently on the big float as the bait runs through. You will see from fig. 12B that all the weight is locked up in the single olivette fixed just 20 in above the hook, with a No. 1 or 3 shot set halfway between them.

When the flow is too strong, or the bream only want a static bait (a complete lack of bites suggests this), dispense with weight on the line by adding a 6-in link of heavier line (to alleviate tangles) with a four-turn water knot about 10 in above the hook. To this, tie on a small bomb just heavy enough to hold bottom when you hold the float steady (fig. 12C). The bait then swings forwards enticingly ahead of the bomb, and can be firmly anchored to the bottom with a dust shot fixed 3–4 in from the hook. Do not be alarmed if most of the float's tip gets pushed beneath the surface, leaving the merest suggestion of the tip. Bites will appear all the more decisive. Remember to keep the pole-tip steady and immediately upstream, with a tight line from tip to tip.

For this method I prefer the flick-tip and tie the rig directly to the small ring glued into the end. If big bream are expected, the rig should be made up on 6 lb test, with hooks from size 14 to 12 tied on a lighter 2-ft length of 3 lb test. Larger hooks, size 10 and 8, are better matched to 4 lb test, and when bream are showing a distinct lack of caution I might even tie them direct.

Despite cold water, the bait will be accepted by bream if it can be presented slowly enough. This is the effectiveness of pole fishing, as John proves with this 3 lb plus bream/roach hybrid. It accepted maggots tripping bottom in over 16 ft of water beneath an 8 g, wire-stem float.

Opposite *If you have the presence of mind and, of course, the time to pre-groundbait on the evening before an early morning start, boat fishing can really put you among the bream. However, you need to be quiet.*

BOAT-FISHING

The enjoyment from going afloat to catch bream in both still and running water is enormous. It is often the only way to tackle bream shoals that inhabit areas completely unapproachable from the bank. Such is the situation on my local Norfolk Broads, for instance, most of which are surrounded by peaty, swampy margins with thick beds of tall reeds. Being largely underfished, these areas obviously contain shoals that rarely see a baited hook and invariably provide consistently good sport.

Boat-fishing also permits tempting, overgrown backwaters and other inaccessible parts of river-systems containing bream features ('Location', p. 25) well away from all the popular areas to be reached. So if you own a suitable car-top dinghy, or dinghy plus trailer, or can arrange to hire one wherever you plan to catch bream, give boat-fishing a try.

You need to be very well organized in a boat, and the first consideration should be a pair of heavy mudweights on adequate-length ropes for keeping the boat anchored in windy conditions. There is nothing more irritating than

suddenly to drift away from a feeding shoal of bream because the mudweights are too light.

Sound carries very easily on water, and one slight 'klunck' on the gunnel or seat can be heard by bream hundreds of yards away, so be especially quiet when rowing up to a potential swim prior to lowering the mudweights. Be very deliberate and slow in all your movements from stowing the oars to preparing nets and bait buckets. Take time to make the rods up, and arrange all the large items neatly in the boat either before you set off, or long before you reach the swim. Take along an old piece of carpet or carpet underlay to cover the floorboards, as this will minimize noise. Several hours spent in a boat encourages fidgeting, which in turn creates still more vibrations, so take along a comfortable folding-chair if there is enough room in the boat. If not, use a pad of thick foam on the seats, which in most boats tend to be rather on the low side.

If you are sitting high above the surface, you will be able to control the float more comfortably and effectively, as you can dip the rod-tip and sink the line to counteract surface drift. And exact float control is imperative when out in a boat, facing the elements. Remember that if you keep too tight a line between float and boat, whenever the boat moves back and forwards on the anchor ropes, the bait will be pulled unnaturally along the bottom. For this reason, and assuming the surface will be broken (flat calms for most of the day are quite rare), by far the best rig is the tipped (insert) peacock waggler set-ups in figs. 8A and 8B (p. 81). The lift method in fig. 8C (p. 81) can usually only be used effectively in really calm conditions, and even then you need to hold the rod to counteract the pull of the boat.

To ensure good sport from an early-morning start, try rowing out to pre-bait the swim the night before (see 'Pre-baiting', p. 73–5), not forgetting to mark the swim in some way. It is surprising just how far out you can be when you make a calculated guess as to the exact position of the swim when you return to a large expanse of water, even when you go to the bother of lining up one feature with another on shore. You can construct a marker from a length of cord, with a 2-oz bomb tied to one end and a loaded (self-cocking) pike float on the other end. Drop the marker over the side of the boat once you have scattered the groundbait about. In the morning, as you approach the spot, use binoculars to look for signs of fish movement, or their bubbles, over the groundbait. Be sure to position the boat up and sideways-on to the wind (with a mud-weight at each end) at a reasonable cast length away from the marker so as not to spook the fish. If during the session the bream are feeding so confidently you feel the boat could be repositioned a little closer to them, simply lift the mudweights off the bottom at each end and use the wind to drift silently forwards.

It is always better to fish from further away to start with, because you then have the option of moving closer later, rather than anchoring too close and scaring the fish initially. Don't forget to take the marker home at the end of the session.

A quick word about using keep-nets in boats is in order, because the bream inside feel much happier if they have the entire length of the net to move about in. Attach a cord to the end ring and tie it up to the gunnel, so the net lies fully extended in a horizontal position. You can easily make a keep-net bracket that screws on to the gunnel from a small G-clamp (available from any hardware shop). Drill a ⅜ BSF hole through the top of the bracket that accommodates the keep-net thread and secure with a nut. The top of the net then rests horizontal to the water surface and is ready to hand when the G-clamp is screwed on.

When anchoring in rivers, you should anchor bows-on to the current. To do this, put down the bow mudweight first (if alone in the boat, this is the easier way round), and let out at least several feet more rope than the depth requires. Once the boat comes round to settle steadily, lower the stern weight on a fairly tight rope. Although it is easier with two anglers in the boat to cast and play fish, if you are anchored sideways-on to the flow, this is only possible in very slow currents. Most river authority by-laws contain very definite regulations about how far from the bank you can put down anchors. In most cases, a distance of one boat-length out from the edge is permitted, but check to be absolutely sure as regulations change from one authority to another. When the flow is too strong for standard waggler techniques, use the stret-pegging rig shown in fig. 10B (p. 89), or simply swap over to a quivertip set-up (see 'Quivertipping', p. 112).

LEDGERING

Swingtipping

Conceived by Jack Clayton of Boston to identify the shy bites of Fenland bream, the swingtip is, in theory, the most sensitive ledgering bite indicator ever invented. However, I must confess to using it rarely, because it does not suit the majority of waters I fish, and because I cannot stand it flapping around on the end of the rod. However, you should not let this influence your opinion of them. Because the swingtip screws into the tip-ring and hangs down in front of the rod, resistance to a biting fish is minimal compared to quivertips, ledger bobbins or monkey climbers. And in certain circumstances, shallow water in particular, bite amplification sometimes occurs; a long swingtip will move further than the distance the bream pulls the bait due to the angle the line follows from the tip to the bait.

It is important to remember that swingtips are only effective in still and very slow-moving water. In fact to counteract even the slightest current, you need to use a loaded swingtip to which weight has been added. For most stillwater situations, except when strong winds rip down the lake or pit causing a heavy undertow, a standard, lightweight swingtip is ideal (see 'Swingtips', p. 48).

Swingtips are great indicators to use when bream-fishing on hard-fished waters. They are also good for registering bites that occur on the drop within seconds of the ledger bomb or feeder hitting the bottom – a common occurrence during high summer, when bream tend to layer off bottom above the feed. The best rig (as it is for all bream ledgering) is the simple fixed paternoster. For this, join a 3–5 ft lighter hook link to the 3–4 lb reel line 12 in above the bomb or feeder, which should be tied direct to the line using a four-turn water knot (fig. 13).

After casting, put the rod in the rests quickly and tighten up to the bomb, watching that tip like a hawk. It will slowly drop backwards after each turn of the reel handle until the line is reasonably tight from bomb to rod. A bite on the drop is easily registered by the tip failing to ease back when it should, because a bream has sucked in the bait and stopped the process.

Buoyant baits such as casters, or a caster and maggot

FIGURE 13 *Fishing on the drop in stillwater with the swingtip*

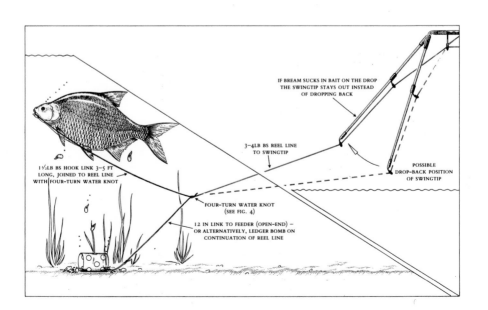

cocktail, are excellent for on the drop fishing. To engineer as slow a fall as possible, use a long, light hook length – about 1½ lb test – and a small, fine-wire hook. Because they are so small and light, size 20 and 22 hooks holding a single maggot fall very slowly indeed.

Once the bait has settled on the bottom and a bream moves directly away from the rod with it, the tip will respond in a positive upwards movement, often straightening out horizontal with the top joint. On other occasions, the tip will rise or suddenly fall no more than ¼ in; treat these as positive bite indications, as though float-fishing. After all, if the float-tip with just ¼ in showing above the surface suddenly disappeared, you would strike and expect to hit into a bream. Ledgering, like float fishing, is all about using the correct indicator for the occasion, and interpreting each movement correctly.

When bites are coming thick and fast, do not bother with rod-rests. Get used to holding the rod handle comfortably beneath your forearm with the tip pointing directly at the bait (fig. 14A). Bites become much easier to see if you allow the rod-tip to angle downwards so that the swingtip is just an inch or so above the surface. Then strike upwards in one smooth, sweeping action. Any abrupt movement could wrap the swingtip around the rod-tip if you miss the bite. When bites are not happening with

FIGURE 14 *Striking when swingtipping*

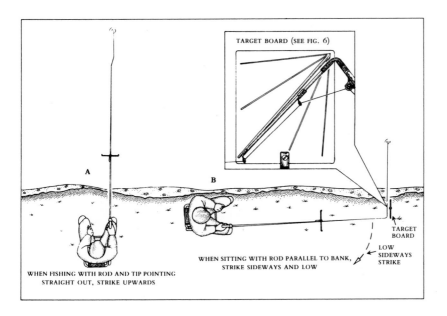

TARGET BOARD (SEE FIG. 6)

A

B

TARGET BOARD

LOW SIDEWAYS STRIKE

WHEN SITTING WITH ROD PARALLEL TO BANK, STRIKE SIDEWAYS AND LOW

WHEN FISHING WITH ROD AND TIP POINTING STRAIGHT OUT, STRIKE UPWARDS

regularity, or it is too cold to hold the rod and concentrate, or bites are barely discernable movements, set the rod on two rests at an angle parallel to the bank and use a target-board positioned immediately behind the tip (see 'Swing-tips', p. 48). Bites, even tiny indications, show up surprisingly well, and to strike you simply ease the rod from the rests in one long, sweeping sideways pull all the way backwards, pulling the line through the water as you would a waggler on a sunk line, not lifting it up against the surface tension, which greatly reduces the effectiveness of the strike (see fig. 14B).

Consistent accuracy in casting is imperative when swingtipping, so on every cast concentrate on putting the bait into the feed area. The only exception to this is when the swim is so full of moving bream that line bites occur on almost every cast. Possessing such incredibly deep bodies and large fins, bream cannot help but pick up the line when they are tightly packed. The swingtip might suddenly flip up and drop back with equal speed – obvious line bites these – or it could straighten out, to all intents and purposes like a positive bite.

Eventually you will learn to distinguish between liners and genuine bites, but whenever you strike and miss what looked to be a positive bite, don't waste time winding in to inspect the bait. Drop the rod-tip immediately after striking and allow the rig to settle again. Besides, now the rig will be closer to you, in a less populated part of the shoal where line bites should be minimal. In fact, casts made to where you consider the outer edge of the feeding shoal to be, as opposed to the centre, are a good plan of attack. You experience less bites, but they are invariably positive lifts resulting in hooked bream, instead of the constant irritation of liners (see 'Line Bites', p. 124–5). In addition, bream hooked on the perimeter of the shoal and bullied quickly away will never spook the others, whereas a big fish hooked from the most dense part of the shoal and then played for several minutes through the others while they are trying to feed, might just unsettle them.

Remember that during the warmer months when the bream's metabolic rate is high and it feeds aggressively, it will consume vast quantities of both loose and cereal feed. This results in the densest part of a large shoal moving position every few minutes. Adjust your casting accordingly.

Martin Founds and Terry Smith of Anglers World Holidays have spent many years researching the best bream fishing areas in southern Ireland. This fantastic catch from the Joinery Stretch of Ballyquirk Lakes at Moycullen came to the feeder in conjunction with bunches of brandling worms.

Quivertipping

Used in conjunction with an open-ended swimfeeder filled with dampened breadcrumbs, quivertipping is the most deadly and versatile method of ledgering for bream in both still and running water, all season through.

For many fishermen, it has completely taken over from the swingtip in recent years due to the wonderful choice of specialist, built-in quivertip rods now available. For close-in work – canals and the like – there are super-sensitive, 7–9 ft wands. At the opposite end of the scale, powerful 11–12 ft feeder rods are available. These are capable of detecting the tiniest bite on a finely-tapered tip from the swirling waters of a weir-pool, but have enough backbone to subdue any size of bream – and even a barbel should you hook one. If you do not wish to own lots of specialist rods, a 10 ft multitip quiver rod with a choice of three or four interchangeable tips (kept in the handle) is the answer (see 'Ledger/Quivertip rods', p. 37–9). However, whatever you decide upon, it is the very tip that you must keep your eyes concentrated on, and you must learn to interpret its every movement so that you can distinguish the difference between weed on the line, line bites, current pull and, of course, a genuine bite.

Quivertipping in running water

The main difference to consider between quivertipping in still and in flowing water is the influence of pressure on the line. In really fast currents, unless you support the rod in two rests with the tip up in the air to keep most of the line above the surface, the tip will be pulled right round by current pressure alone. This completely defeats the object of having a finely-tapered tip in the first place. Moreover, when current pressure becomes too great, the bomb or feeder will bounce off downstream and in towards the bank along the bottom, dragging the bait well away from the intended swim.

I well remember fishing the fabulous River Guden in Denmark along with my old buddy, Terry Smith from Sheffield, during one of the international *Go Fishing* television programmes. Our only chance of contacting the bream we so badly needed for the programme was to cast over to the opposite side of a wide bay into a shallow slack where they were congregating (we happened to be on the wrong side of the river). The main flow between the bream and our bank was going at an incredible speed. It seemed an almost impossible situation. Yet we managed to overcome the problem by using very long, extending rod-rests that kept our 12-ft quivertip rods so high they were almost vertical. In fact, I soon developed severe neck-ache from continually looking skywards at the tip. But this solved the problem admirably, so long as the feeder held in the slack and kept the line out of the main flow. Most bites to our corn-and-worm cocktails were dramatic drop backs, and once those Guden bream got into the main flow we had a real fight on our hands bringing them back upstream. It was made even more difficult by the dense beds of incredibly tall common reed lining the margins. We fished from narrow swims cut into these reed-beds, providing no downstream view whatsoever, and the first time we saw anything of each bream was when it was ready for the net.

What fabulous, hard-fighting bream they are in the River Guden; but then, bream from fast, clear waters put enormous torque on the line once they turn their deep flanks side-on to the current, wherever you catch them. They pose a great challenge. In slow-moving rivers, where current pressure creates minimal torque on the line, always position the rod angled downwards with the tip as close to the surface as is practical. This greatly improves your view of the tip, and alleviates the effect of wind resistance on the line.

I prefer quivertipping for bream in weir-pools. I love the challenge they offer, both summer and winter. During levels of low oxygen in other parts of the river, when drought conditions may prevail at the end of the summer, weir-pools can fill up with quality bream. Very often at this time of year they prefer to occupy the shallow, bubbly water along a fast run immediately beneath a sluice. In these situations, heavy feeding is not required. Catapult a regular supply of hook-bait fragments into the head of the run so they come to settle on the gravel among the shoal, which can often be seen through polaroid glasses in the fast water. Corn and worms are my favourite summer weir-

pool baits, with large lumps of bread flake in reserve. The tip should be held high after casting to alleviate undue pressure on the line, enabling you to hold bottom with the minimum of weight. A small bomb, or better still a string of swan shots on the link of a fixed paternoster rig, is ideal because it is so easy to add or take away shots to achieve that fine balance (fig. 15A). Then concentrate on the quivertip for the gentle drop-back as the bream sucks in the bait. If allowed to develop, the bite might well register as an unmissable pull round on the tip as the bream angles off downstream with the bait. However, fast-water bream like to keep their position and could quickly drop the bait on feeling resistance. Always look for drop-backs as the first indication of a strikeable bite. Sometimes the tip merely vibrates or shakes – again this is a strikeable bite. Small, sharp 'plinks' on the rod tip invariably turn out to be line bites or small nuisance fish like gudgeon mouthing the bait.

During the winter months, when bream will have retreated to the deeper, slower parts of the pool and are nowhere near so aggressive, particularly in really cold

Often, the only way of contacting bream inhabiting the swirling waters of deep mill and weir pools, is to present a static bait hard on the bottom. John puts his Avon quivertip rod through its paces in this Norfolk pool, as a bream turns side on to the current and heads downstream.

Opposite *When quivertip ledgering in running water, the secret for alleviating current pressure against the line is to position the rod-tip high, thus keeping most of the line clear of the water.*

FIGURE 15 *Weirpool*
quivertipping

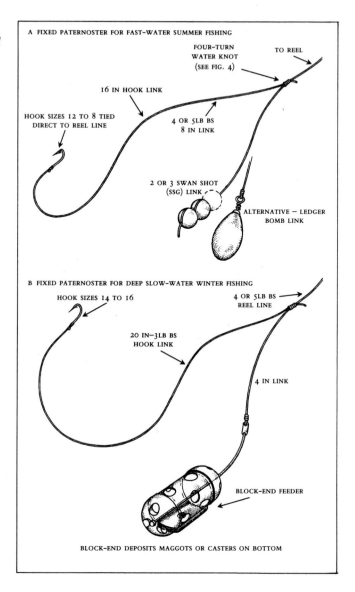

A FIXED PATERNOSTER FOR FAST-WATER SUMMER FISHING

FOUR-TURN
WATER KNOT
(SEE FIG. 4)

TO REEL

16 IN HOOK LINK

HOOK SIZES 12 TO 8 TIED
DIRECT TO REEL LINE

4 OR 5LB BS
8 IN LINK

2 OR 3 SWAN SHOT
(SSG) LINK

ALTERNATIVE — LEDGER
BOMB LINK

B FIXED PATERNOSTER FOR DEEP SLOW-WATER WINTER FISHING

HOOK SIZES 14 TO 16

4 OR 5LB BS
REEL LINE

20 IN–3LB BS
HOOK LINK

4 IN LINK

BLOCK-END FEEDER

BLOCK-END DEPOSITS MAGGOTS OR CASTERS ON BOTTOM

periods, I reduce hooks to sizes 14–16 tied to a 3 lb hook
link and turn to maggots and casters, depositing them on
the bottom with a block-end feeder (fig. 15B). Only in
mild spells do I increase the hook size to, say, a 10 and offer
large baits such as a lobworm or lump of bread flake.
When quivertipping in deep rivers with a steady but slow
push of water, the same technique of small hook sizes and a
block-end feeder should be used, even during the hours of
darkness.

Quivertipping at night

Quivertipping is as effective for taking big catches throughout the night in running water as float-fishing is on stillwaters. In order to concentrate without eye strain I prefer to illuminate the tip with a powerful, narrow torch-beam. I position it a few feet downstream, and angle it upwards towards the rod so that it shines only on the tip and not on the surface of the water. Night vision is then in no way impaired – nor is the feeding shoal spooked (fig. 16).

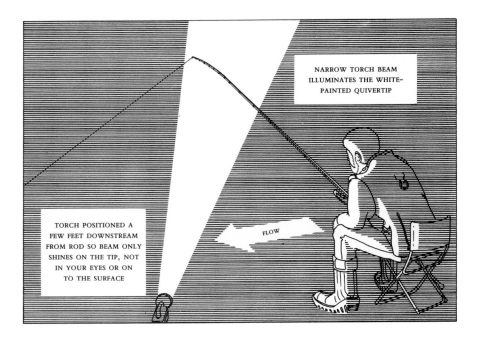

NARROW TORCH BEAM ILLUMINATES THE WHITE-PAINTED QUIVERTIP

TORCH POSITIONED A FEW FEET DOWNSTREAM FROM ROD SO BEAM ONLY SHINES ON THE TIP, NOT IN YOUR EYES OR ON TO THE SURFACE

FLOW

FIGURE 16
Quivertipping at
night in running water

A torch may be more expensive than a luminous starlight or betalight element fixed to the tip, but provided the last 20 in of the tip is painted matt white – to reflect the torch beam – you can fish for hour upon hour in a pleasant, relaxed manner. Incidentally, the tips of all my quivertips are painted white. I find that even during daylight, especially in low light, it is by far the easiest colour to see against a variety of backgrounds. If white does not work for you, try fluorescent matt yellow.

Tighten up to the bait perhaps a little more than you

If you support the rod butt comfortably across your thigh, while keeping the top half of the rod steady on a telescopic rod rest with the quivertip mere inches above the surface, you have maximum stability for interpreting the tiniest of bites when stillwater ledgering.

would during daylight (and use a heavier feeder), so the tip has a definable curve. Drop-back bites then become apparent immediately.

When fishing new swims, it is well worth doing some pre-baiting to ensure that you do not waste a night's sleep (see 'Pre-baiting', p. 73–5).

Stillwater quivertipping

Generally speaking, bites in static water are not going to register on the tip as boldly as those in running water, so opt for a finely-tapered, super-sensitive tip. If using screw-in tips, one of 1½ oz test curve is suitable, although in extremely cold weather a step down to a 1 oz tip will improve bite registration.

To alleviate wind disturbance, position the rod on two rests (I use a front one only and rest the rod butt on my right knee for a quick strike) with the tip just a couple of inches above the surface – where, incidentally, bites show up better. Angle the rod to either left or right (whichever is more comfortable) and follow through along the same line on the strike. If the water is very deep, strike upwards; if it is shallow strike low to the water (see fig. 17).

FIGURE 17
Quivertipping in stillwater

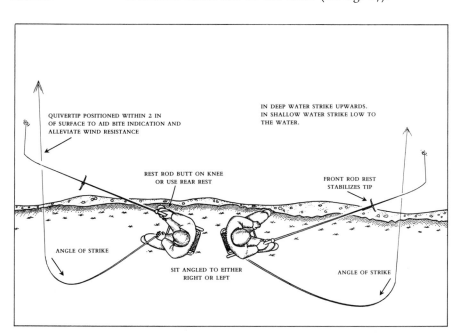

IN DEEP WATER STRIKE UPWARDS.
IN SHALLOW WATER STRIKE LOW TO
THE WATER.

QUIVERTIP POSITIONED WITHIN 2 IN
OF SURFACE TO AID BITE INDICATION AND
ALLEVIATE WIND RESISTANCE

REST ROD BUTT ON KNEE
OR USE REAR REST

FRONT ROD REST
STABILIZES TIP

ANGLE OF STRIKE

SIT ANGLED TO EITHER
RIGHT OR LEFT

ANGLE OF STRIKE

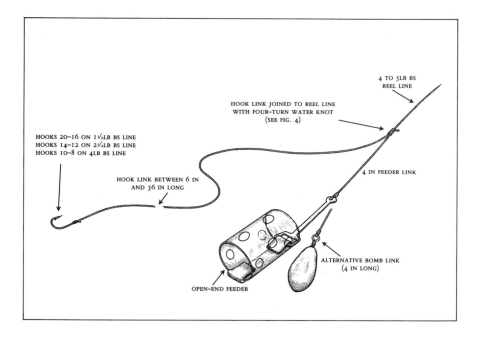

4 TO 5LB BS
REEL LINE

HOOK LINK JOINED TO REEL LINE
WITH FOUR-TURN WATER KNOT
(SEE FIG. 4)

HOOKS 20–16 ON 1½LB BS LINE
HOOKS 14–12 ON 2½LB BS LINE
HOOKS 10–8 ON 4LB BS LINE

HOOK LINK BETWEEN 6 IN
AND 36 IN LONG

4 IN FEEDER LINK

ALTERNATIVE BOMB LINK
(4 IN LONG)

OPEN-END FEEDER

FIGURE 18
Quivertipping – fixed paternoster feeder rig for still or running water

The end rig is the faithful fixed paternoster, with a bomb on the end if you wish to loose-feed by catapult or groundbait by hand only. Substitution of an open-end swimfeeder for the bomb, however, dramatically increases the chances of immediate bites because it deposits a pile of crumb and bait fragments right where it matters alongside the hook bait (see fig. 18).

Note how the hook length is tied to the reel line and varies in test according to the hook size. This in turn is dictated by the bait and to some extent by the size of bream expected. When using maggots, for example, start with a 3 ft hook link, but if they return sucked to skins without a bite registering, start reducing the hook link until hittable movements are seen on the tip. Sometimes bream run along the bottom with the bait and pull the tip slowly all the way round. At other times they chew the bait on the spot, showing only the merest indication on the tip.

You can often create a response by winding in gently a half or one full turn of the reel handle, should the bream think its food is getting away. And this ruse works especially well when baiting with worms. I am sure it is the gyrating movement of the worms, plus their internal juices, which really excite bream. On another day they might refuse worms, corn or maggots, and show interest only in fluffy, white bread flake. So always be prepared to experiment when bites are not forthcoming. Change baits, use cocktails and move the bait along every so often to goad them into grabbing hold of it.

The importance of bait movement was well and truly brought home to me during a spell of research and film-making for the Irish Tourist Board in the company of my old pal, Terry Smith on the lakes at Moycullen a few years back. Being April, and with the water cold, a good 90 per cent of the bites came only when our bunches of worms were inched slowly along the bottom. If the bait was left static, those bream showed little interest.

Watch out for the tip slowly but decisively dropping back, a sure sign the bream has moved towards the rod and in so doing has dislodged the feeder. To encourage drop-back bites, use just enough lead on the feeder to enable you to tighten up after casting but not so much the bream will drop the bait again. The only situations on stillwaters when I would use more lead than is necessary are either to aid casting, or to get the bait down quickly through deep water, past the attentions of nuisance shoal fish like roach and rudd to the bream feeding on the bottom.

Whenever you can, get used to holding the rod and support it on the front rest only; and make sure the line will lift off cleanly at whichever angle you strike. This way, you can make small movements of the bait, and reply to snatchy bites, much more easily. Dampen the bread-crumbs going into the feeder only very lightly so they explode as it touches bottom, sending a cascade of attractive feed all around the hook bait. If the breadcrumbs are too wet they could clog the feeder, and remain inside it until you pull in for a recast. Loose-feed hook fragments can be added to the crumb, or you can sandwich a quantity of hook baits like maggots, corn or casters, or even finely chopped worms, between a plug of breadcrumbs at each end of the feeder (see 'Feeder Groundbait', p. 73).

At the start of the session it is a good ploy to lob out a few balls of groundbait (stiffened well for throwing) by hand to get the bream feeding. Then keep them interested and moving around within the area through the feeder's regular arrival carrying extra food, whether bites are coming or not. The secret of feeder-fishing is consistency in casting accuracy and introducing those piles of food.

With specimen bream in mind, and his stewed-wheat hookbait presented in conjunction with an open-ended swimfeeder positioned over 60 yd out, in a pre-groundbaited deep gulley, Charlie Clay prepares for a long, sweeping strike as the bobbin indicator rises to the butt ring.

Distance ledgering

When seeking lake or gravel-pit bream at distances of, say,
40 yd plus, and also when after specimen bream, I change
outfits completely. At this distance I use an Avon-
actioned, 11 or 12 ft carbon rod of 1¼ lb test curve (see
'Ledger/quivertip rods', p. 37–9) for maximum line pick-
up, and a 6 lb test line. I also change bite indicators,
switching to the ledger bobbin. This clips on to the line
between butt-ring and reel, and falls harmlessly to the
ground on a retaining cord, even when I make a hard,
sweeping strike. For daytime ledgering I use the
fluorescent-red tenpin bobbin, and after dark the luminous
glo-bobbin, which incorporates a betalight element. The
glo-bobbin can of course be used around the clock.

Whenever long periods of inactivity are likely – for
example on waters where there is a low density of bream
(often the case with 'big-fish-only' lakes and pits), or
during the hours of darkness when long periods of
inactivity are liable to occur – it is comforting to have an
electric alarm incorporated into the set-up, and the
Optonic indicator is ideal. An alarm, or 'buzzer' as they are
called by carp anglers, allows you to appreciate fully the
surrounding wildlife, and also to scan the surface with
binoculars away from the area being fished for signs of
bream activity. Indeed, I wish I had a £5 note for every
bonus fish that has graced the landing-net as a result of
winding in and placing a bait on top of a bream I had seen
breaking the surface. Watching a pair of bobbins (two rods
are an advantage when covering a large area) for hour upon
hour is not just dull; you are missing out on much of the
pleasure that ledgering for bream has to offer. This is a
clear-cut case where electronic wizardry earns its keep.
However, do not turn the volume up so loud that
everyone on the next lake hears it. Apart from the
irritation this causes to other anglers, you are also
informing them of your success. Incidentally, to stop
bobbins blowing about or steadily rising with the underwater tow and registering annoying false bites, pinch two
or three swan shots on to the retaining cord immediately
below the bobbin.

As for rigs, the faithful fixed paternoster ledger is still

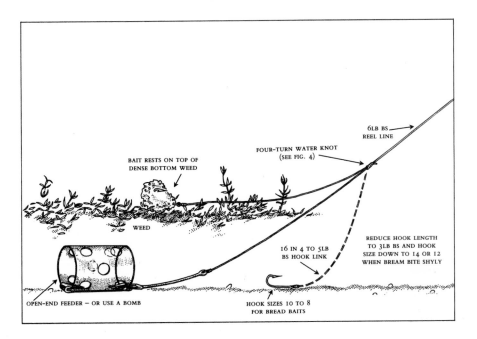

Within the figure:
- 6LB BS REEL LINE
- FOUR-TURN WATER KNOT (SEE FIG. 4)
- BAIT RESTS ON TOP OF DENSE BOTTOM WEED
- WEED
- 16 IN 4 TO 5LB BS HOOK LINK
- REDUCE HOOK LENGTH TO 3LB BS AND HOOK SIZE DOWN TO 14 OR 12 WHEN BREAM BITE SHYLY
- OPEN-END FEEDER – OR USE A BOMB
- HOOK SIZES 10 TO 8 FOR BREAD BAITS

FIGURE 19 *Distance ledgering in stillwater – fixed paternoster*

top of the list, but slightly changed. For distance ledgering, and for presenting baits over thick bottom-weed so they come to rest on top in full view, I use a bomb or feeder link of 4–5 ft and a hook link of around 16–20 in joined to the reel line with a four-turn water knot (see fig. 19).

Where only small numbers of large bream are present and regular helpings of groundbait are not required. I usually put out a few balls by catapult and stick to a bomb ledger. On the other hand, where there are large shoals capable of continually mopping up loose feed and crumb groundbait, the open-ended swimfeeder is indispensable, especially when you are casting distances beyond accurate catapult range.

The further out you present the bait, the greater will be the problems of setting the hook, especially a large hook, so remember to follow through on the strike in a full, scything movement, keeping the angle at which the line is lying beneath the surface. For instance, in shallow water strike sideways and low to the water, pulling the line through it. If you strike upwards, the effective power of the strike will be reduced by the surface tension on the water. In very deep water, where the line angles straight down away from the rod tip, an upward strike is required.

As bream become aware of what's going on and bites are

The rewards of quivertip ledgering. A wonderful bag of bream to over 7 lb shared by Dave Thomas and John from the fabulous River Shannon between Portumna and Meelick.

indicated by mere 3–4 in lifts of the bobbin, plus the odd seemingly-unhittable twitch, try doing two things. Reduce the hook length from 16–20 in down to 6–8 in, and stand up behind the rods ready to hit any slight movements of the bobbins.

A step down in hook and bait size and in the strength, or more importantly the diameter, of the hook length, will also help to promote more confidence from the bream and consequently more positive, hittable bites. At the beginning of the season I may present large lumps of bread flake on size 6 hooks tied direct to 6 lb test. By mid-July, however, in order to continue catching, I will have stepped down to size 14 hooks on a 3 lb hook link and switched over to corn, wheat, casters, maggots or brandlings. And this is with specimen bream in mind. For smaller fish you should step down further in hook and bait size, with a mind to switching baits and swims once the bream have become aware of your presence. Shoal fish like bream are creatures of habit, and when one that has itself been recently caught or spooked sees its neighbour refuse what looks to be a perfectly good meal, it is all the more unlikely to feed on the same bait presented in the same spot.

LINE BITES

Let me conclude with a few words about line bites, which are a problem throughout the season. Even during the early season when fish should have finished spawning, bream in stillwaters may still be going through the motions of their reproductive cycle as late as the beginning of July if there has been a late spring. They will be chasing each other about, the males plainly recognizable by the white spawning tubercles covering their heads and shoulders. This adds to the fisherman's frustration, because not only are the majority not particularly interested in feeding, but they will also be continually bumping into his line and registering seemingly-unmissable, sailaway bites on the bobbin. Incidentally, if you are missing bites cast after cast and are unsure whether they are line bites or real bites, cast out without any bait on the hook.

I mentioned earlier that casts short of the baited area, to

the very edge of the shoal, can help alleviate the line-bite problem. So too does angling the rod-tip down several inches beneath the surface, to reduce the angle at which the line is suspended between bait and rod. Nonetheless, you will experience occasions, whether ledgering, float-fishing or even freelining, when odd groups of bream still manage to hit the line and register false bites. It is all part and parcel of summer bream fishing, so you will have to continue tearing your hair out or invest in a set of golf-clubs.

Good bream fishing

INDEX

Avon, River, Hampshire 28–9
baits 58–75
  bread 59–62
  groundbaiting 68–73, 117
  natural 62–6
  particles 66–8
  pre-baiting 73–5
  in still and slow-moving
    water 94
Bann, River, Northern Ireland 18,
  97
Beeston Lake, Norfolk 12
bite indicators 52–3, 120
  see also swingtipping
bloodworms 21
boat-fishing 98–101
bobbin indicators 52, 120
Bows, Ray 32–3
bread 59–62
  groundbaiting 69–71, 117
bream (bronze, Abramis
    brama) 9–14
  baits 58–75
  coloration 9–10
  distribution of 20
  feeding 15–21, 23, 26
  location of 21–35
  reproduction 16–20
  size 10–13
  tackle 36–57
  techniques and rigs 76–125
  young 9
Bromley, Anthony 12
bubbles, feeding 15, 33
Butler, Malcolm 32

Cambridgeshire 20, 33–5
canals, locating bream 33–5
casters 64–5
centre-pin reels 39–40
Chiddingstone Castle Lake 12
Clayton, Jack 102
Clegg, Dick 28–9
coloration, bream 9–10
  hybrids 17
  silver bream 19–20
colour of water 9–10, 33
Costin, E. 12
crumbs, bread 69–70, 72–3, 117
crust, bread 61–2

Davison, Mike 12
distance ledgering 120–4
distribution of bream 20

eggs 16

elasticated tips 37, 93
electric bite alarms/buzzers 52–3,
  120

feeder groundbait 73
feeding 15–21, 23, 26
  at night 35, 85
Fens, locating bream 33–5
fins 9–10
fixed paternoster rig 116, 120–1
fixed-spool reels 40–1
flake, bread 60, 109
flick-tip fishing 46
float rods 36–7
floats 45–8

glo-bobbins 120
gravel pits 21–3
groundbaiting 68–73, 117
Guden, River, Denmark 108–9

hempseed, stewed 71
hit-and-hold tactics, pole-
  fishing 96
hooks 41–2
hybridization 17–18

insert peacock waggler rig 79–81,
  100

keep-nets 56–7
  in boats 101
knots 42–5

landing-nets 53–6
laying-on, with waggler 91–2
ledger rods 37–9
ledgering 102–24
  distance 120–4
  quivertipping 108–17
  reels 40–1
  swingtipping 102–7
  see also quivertips; swingtips
lift method, waggler-style floatfishing 84–5
lilies 35, 91
line bites 28, 107, 124–5
lines 41
locating bream 21–35
  canals and the Fens 33–5
  feeding 15–16
  rivers 25, 26–30
  stillwaters 21–6
  weir-pools 20, 31–3

maggots 62–4, 75
Meelick 32
Moycullen 117

mucus layer 9
multi-tip quiver rod 38, 108

natural baits 62–6
  casters 64–5
  maggots 62–4, 75
  worms 65–6, 109
night fishing 35
  bite indicators 52–3, 120
  lift method waggler 84–5
  pre-baiting 24
  quivertipping 113–14
night-light tips 85
Norfolk Broads 12, 13, 18, 24, 98

Old Bedford River,
  Cambridgeshire 20

particle baits 66–8
paste, bread 60–1
polaroid glasses 31
pole-fishing 93–7
  deep flowing water 96–7
  hit-and-hold tactics 96
  still and slow-moving
    water 93–4
poles 37
  floats 46
  tips 46–8
pollution 13
pre-baiting 24, 58
  baits 73–5

Queenford Lagoon, Thames
  Valley 12
quivertip rods 37–9
quivertipping 108–17
  at night 113–14
  in running water 108–12
  in stillwaters 114–17
  weir-pools 112
quivertips 38, 51

reels 39–41
reproduction 16–20
reservoirs 21
rice 71
rigs see techniques and rigs
rivers
  locating bream 25, 26–30
  pole-fishing 96–7
  quivertipping 108–12
  waggler-style floatfishing 85–91
roach/bream hybrids 17–18
rods 36–9
  float 36–7
  ledger/quivertips 37–9
  poles 37
rover fishing 33–4
Royalty Fishery, Christchurch 28
rudd/bream hybrids 17
running ledger rigs 44

Shannon, River, Irish
  Republic 26, 32, 96–7

silver bream 19–20
size, bream 10–13
slime layer 9
Smith, Terry 108–9, 117
spawning 16
starlights 84–5, 113
stillwater green rig 76–9
stillwaters 20
  coloured 9
  depth of 21–4
  locating bream 21–6
  pole-fishing 93–4
  quivertipping 114–17
stret-pegging 89, 91
swan shots 91–2
sweetcorn 68, 109
swingtipping 102–7
swingtips 38, 48–51

tackle 36–57
  bite indicators 52–3, 120
  floats 45–8
  hooks 41–2
  keep-nets 56–7
  knots 42–5
  landing-nets 53–6
  lines 41
  quivertips 38, 51
  reels 39–41
  rods 36–9
  swingtips 38, 48–51
techniques and rigs 76–125
  boat-fishing 98–101
  ledgering 102–24
  line bites 124–5
  pole-fishing 93–7
  waggler-style floatfishing
    76–92
teeth 15
tipped (insert) peacock waggler
  rig 79–81, 100
tips
  elasticated 37, 93
  night-light 85
  see also quivertips; swingtips
torches 113
twin-tip ledger rod 39

waggler-style floatfishing 76–92
  laying-on 91–2
  lift method 84–5
  in-moving water 85–91
  stillwater green rig 76–9
  tipped (insert) peacock rig 79–81,
    100
water-lilies 35, 91
weir-pools 20, 31–3
  quivertipping 112
wheat, stewed 66–7, 71
winter
  locating bream 31–2
  quivertipping 111–12
worms 65–6, 109

FATHER & SON

The world's biggest selling angling weekly publication has now launched the best selling fishing monthly. So join the family and get the best of both worlds...the latest news and views every Wednesday in *Angling Times*...the top advice and instruction in *Improve Your Coarse Fishing* every month.

Everything you need to know about coarse fishing is covered by these two publications...they make the perfect combination.

The No I for.......
- Form guides
- Latest tackle reviews
- Hot news stories
- Fishery spotlights
- Match reports
- Features

The No I for.......
- Hints and tips
- Facts on bait
- Species spotlights
- Fish-catching rigs
- In-depth tackle trials
- Which guides